Tessa Newcomb's
Paris

Tessa Newcomb's
Paris

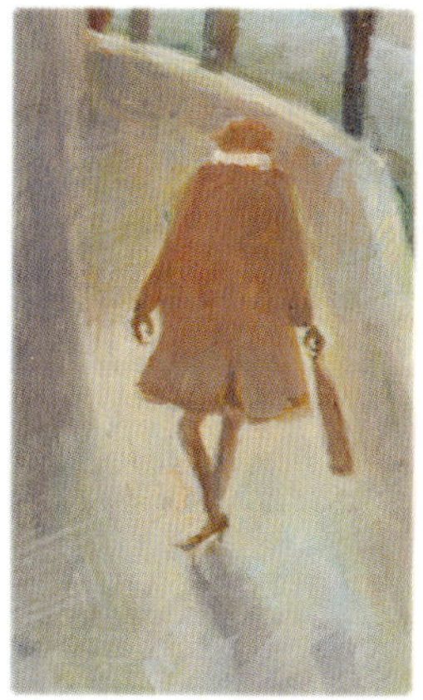

Edited with Foreword
by Philip Vann

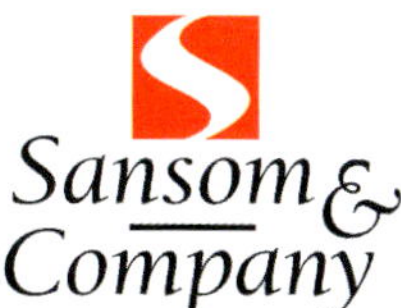

Sansom &
Company

Acknowledgements

The author would like to thank Philip Vann, Bob Jackson,
Henry Jackson Newcomb, Telfer Stokes, Ken Skipper and Douglas
Atfield for their helpful contributions to the making of this book.

First published in 2014 by Sansom & Company Ltd.,
81g Pembroke Road, Bristol BS8 3EA

info@sansomandcompany.co.uk
www.sansomandcompany.co.uk

© Tessa Newcomb and Philip Vann

ISBN 978-1-908326-53-9

British Library Cataloguing-in-Publication Data
A catalogue record for this book is available from the British Library

set in Minion Pro 10.5
Design and typesetting by Stephen Morris, www.stephen-morris.co.uk
Printed and bound in the Czech Republic via Akcent Media

Contents

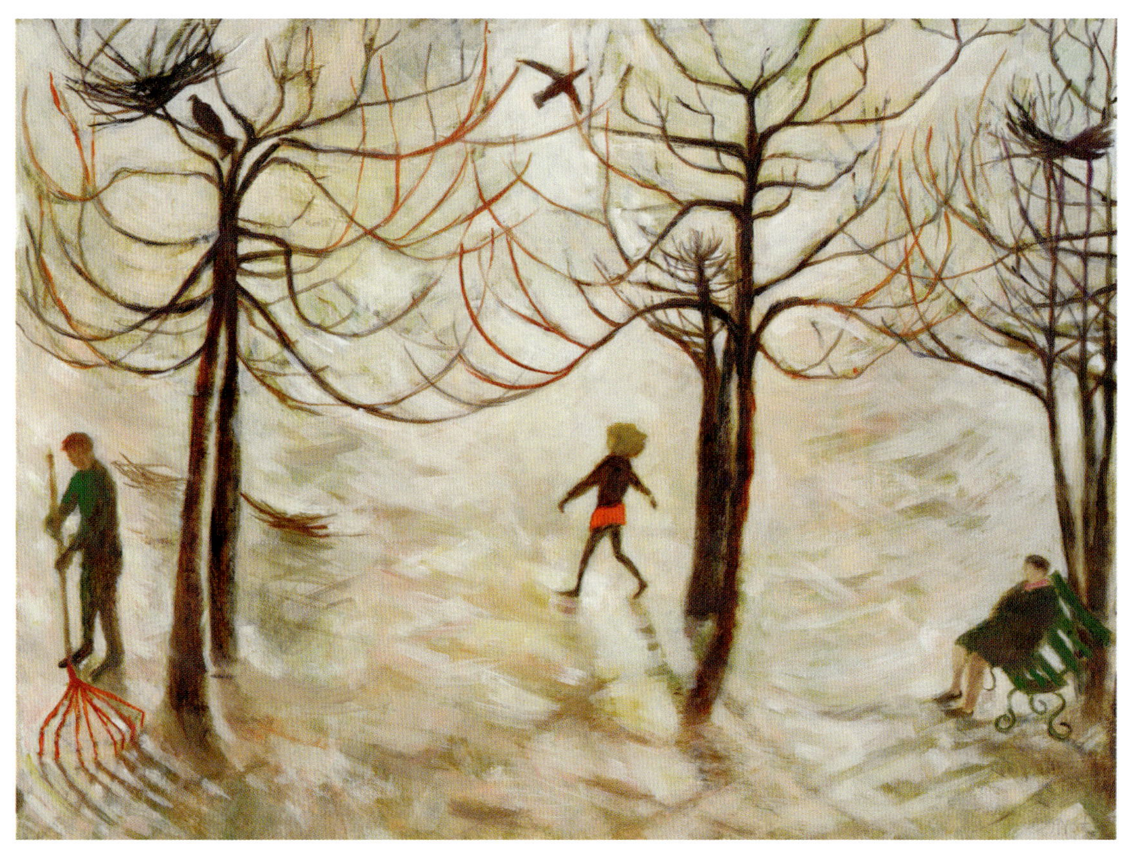

Self-Portrait, 2007
oil on board
18 x 24 inches

Foreword

Since Tessa Newcomb first ventured to Paris aged sixteen, she has enjoyed occasional, brief visits there, during which she stores up, and sketches, innumerable impressions – starting points for paintings made later in her Suffolk studio – which portray a wide metropolitan gamut of *luxe et misère, haute couture* and *gamine chic, haute cuisine* of delicious artistry and 'simple little restaurants, where the bill of fare is written on the slate and where the smell of fried onions always hangs in the air' (in Georges Simenon's words). These *vignettes* are further layered with the flavour of Tessa's own eclectic reading of writers inspired by Paris, including Verlaine, Hope Mirrlees, Katherine Mansfield, Cocteau, Colette, Jean Rhys and Françoise Sagan, and informed by the sublimely *soigné* perspectives of Atget's multi-faceted early twentieth-century photographic views of the city.

In her radically innovative 1919 poem *Paris*, Hope Mirrlees evoked 'Little funny things ceaselessly happening' on odiferous boulevards and under a saffron-coloured sky just as *les Halles* is about to open. Similarly, Tessa depicts the city's *flanêurs*, expectant lovers, dainty eaters of patisserie, stall-holders selling mushrooms, mobile phone users outside cafés, butchers cleaning up and chess players sequestered under trees in the Luxembourg Gardens.

In a letter (dated 10 May 1922), Katherine Mansfield recalled,

The weather is really divine. I spent yesterday in the Bois at a marvellous place… You can't imagine how beautifully these women dance in the open under the flowering chestnut trees to a delicious band. All the very height of luxury. I do like luxury – just for a dip in and out of. Especially in Paris because it's made into such an Art.

Tessa also enjoys dipping in and out of the rarefied luxury of Paris – but like Mansfield herself, she is aware that is just one (if supremely, divinely exquisite) side of the city.

On her visits to Paris, Tessa has tended to stay in modest hotel rooms and doubtless concurs with the novelist Jean Rhys's finding that Paris can be an opulently beguiling place but also a city of an almost fearsome existential loneliness which may serve to encourage a freshly heightened, detached view of things. One of Rhys's characters, a young Englishwoman, staying in a run-down hotel just before the Second World War, ruminates:

This musty smell, the bugs, the loneliness, this room, which is part of the street outside – this is all I want from life.

Tessa Newcomb's own poignantly and wittily nuanced writings and paintings about Paris similarly encompass the extremes, as well as the quotidian epiphanies, of this most beautiful, paradoxical and richly contradictory city.

Philip Vann, May 2014

How I see Paris

Ah! la charmante chose Ah! It is a charming thing

Quitter un pays morose To depart from a dreary land

Pour Paris For Paris

Paris joli Beautiful Paris

from 'Voyage à Paris' by Guillaume Apollinaire (1880-1918)

I paint Paris how I want it to look. A Paris drawn from films, books, poems. Fewer cars, less noise and stress, better clothes, nicer notice boards – or that's what I like to imagine. I use selective vision.

My first trip to Paris was with my mother, the painter Mary Newcomb. I think she wanted someone to go with. I was sixteen and had not been out of Suffolk much. On the first day we went straight to the cinema of the Musée d'Art Moderne. As the doors opened one's eye was immediately taken to the black centre of Sonia Delaunay's 1914 painting *Electric Prisms*, swirling around simultaneous circles – and we looked at a Cubist Robert Delaunay painting (from 1910) where the Eiffel Tower burst through the hotel curtains while the modern world revolved around it. I found all this most exciting, and when I got home I applied to art school.

Later I went as a student. This was by overnight ferry. Standing on deck in the 5am dawn as we approached Dieppe was part of the excitement. One arrived later at the Gare du Nord slightly rocking from the boat and the lack of sleep. Then everything seemed grey and smelt of Gauloises. But Paris still felt very fresh to me.

We went to a Chagall exhibition at the Louvre. He was still alive then and these were his new paintings – they had black segments. I did a drawing from the window sill of people crossing the bridge in the snow. It was just before Christmas. We did the trip on £40, making the last packet of biscuits last the journey home.

I like to see Paris as Marquet did in his paintings around 1907. His vantage point is often hovering somewhere above the street so you are observing miniscule people crossing bridges, the occasional horse and cart, boats chugging the Seine with plumes of smoke from their chimney stacks, silent barges, the bookstalls and bare black trees against light water or sky. All clearly defined and delineated – not like the mayhem of today.

You can still find bits of old Paris – go through a door into a yard. We went to this strange café in the Latin Quarter in an

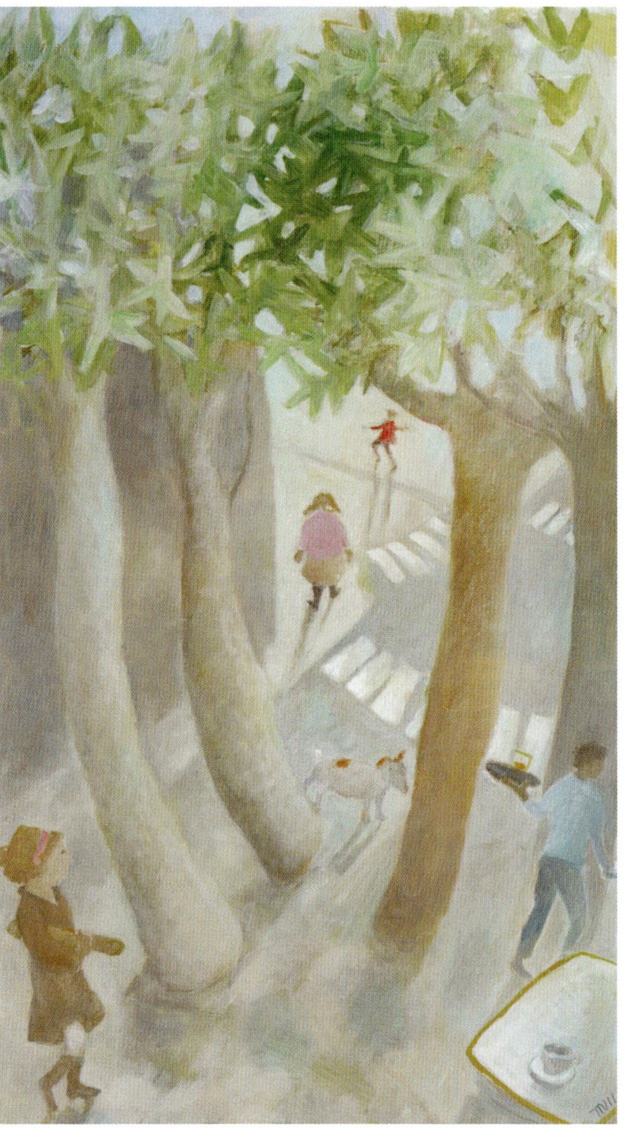

Sunday Morning, 2011, oil on board, 24 x 13½ inches

otherwise smart street. I thought it was Polish at first. Fairly gloomy inside, a few people standing around a bar at the back, a metal spiral staircase, a curtain pulled back over a door. A man with a red scarf thrown over his shoulder hobbled towards us. We ordered rough red wine and a piece of quiche. To go to the lavatory you had to go out into the yard. It was straight from an Atget photograph.

Eugène Atget took hundreds of photographs of Paris in the early twentieth century. Seeing them made me want to return to Paris – to find those places. The photographs are beautiful still compositions, inhabited but without anyone in them.

The streets are empty – he photographed them very early in the morning. The buildings pose.

Back in the café, a small white car parked up on the pavement. A nun rushed in with some croissants, which she gave to a man who was holding forth from one of the tables. Before leaving, she climbed on a chair to wind a grandfather clock.

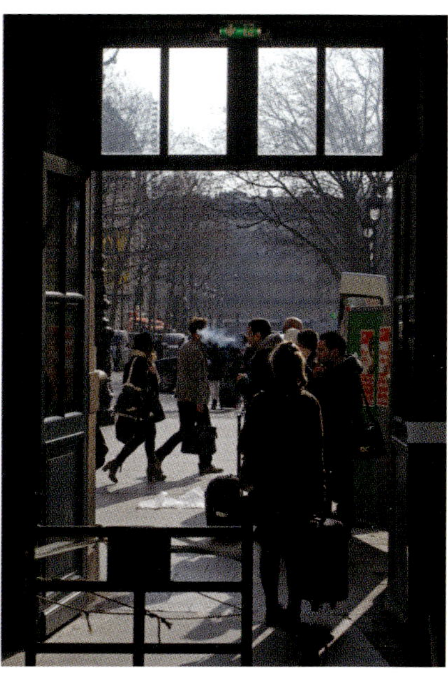

Entrance of the Gare du Nord. Tessa arriving in Paris thinking, 'I must buy some new shoes.'
Photo: Henry Jackson Newcomb

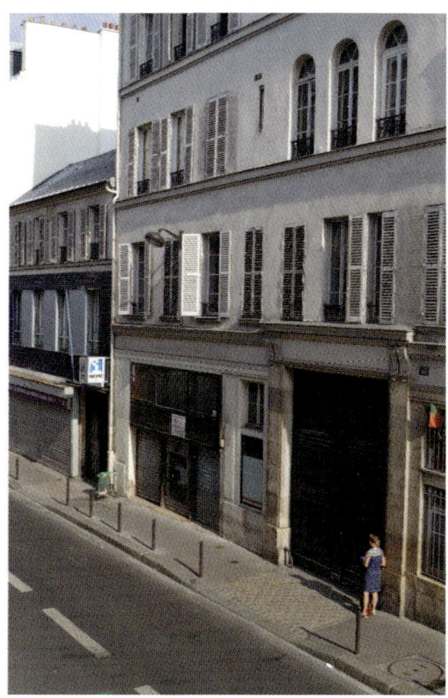

Tessa drawing in the street.
Photo: Henry Jackson Newcomb

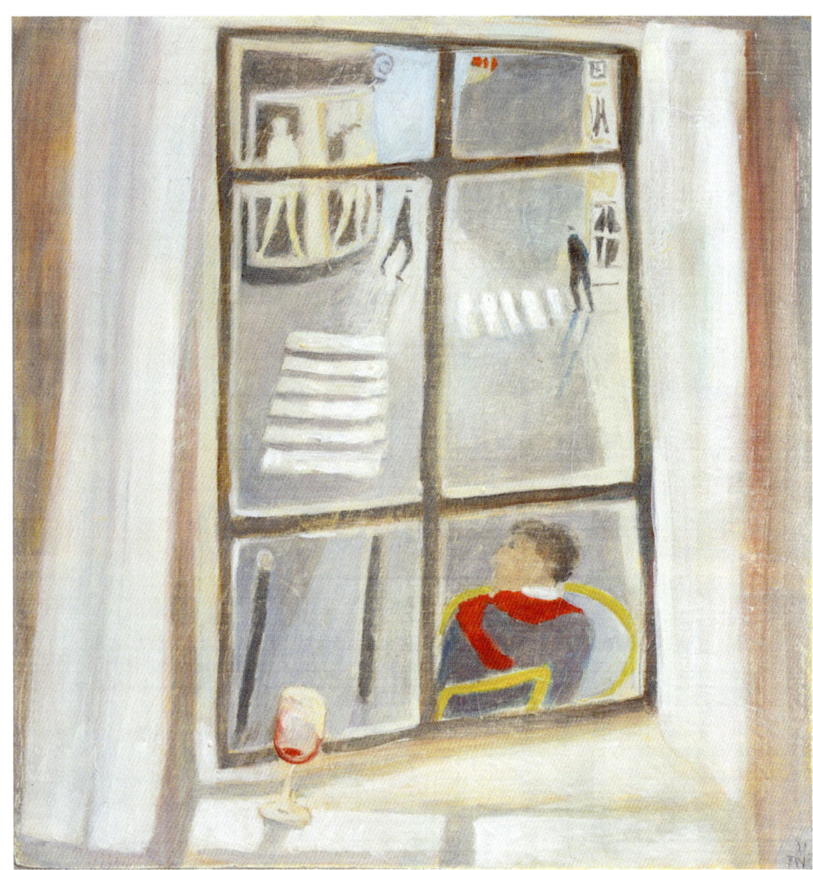

Café (Equations), 2011
oil on board, 12 x 11 inches

Changing

We seem an English crowd as we board the Eurostar, with a smatter-
ing of exotic French. Something happens under the Channel and most
of us arrive feeling more French – but I still feel a bit hopelessly
English. The reverse happens on the way back. We all get out – and
can relax again at being English.

On the train three women take up a lot of
space with their talk of the shopping trip
that they are going on, and other trips that
they have been on. In the fourth seat a
man keeps his elbows pressed to his sides
and reads *L'Art du Bouddhisme*.

Sun racing by–
golden on Old Man's Beard.
Bruise-coloured clouds.

The sea used to separate us from France.
Now it's seamless – but if you look out of
the train window you will see the pylons
are of a different design.
Past miles of graffiti, drawing into the
Gare du Nord, Parisian houses arise.

I came to draw but I've no pencil and
they've confiscated my Stanley knife.

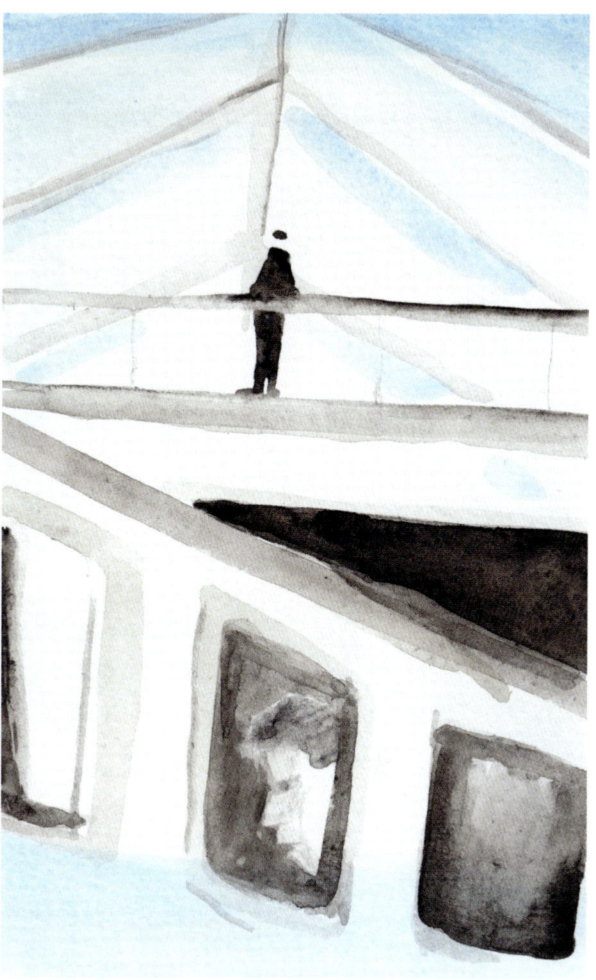

Leaving, 2012, watercolour, 7½ x 5 inches

Colour

To me Paris is female. An elderly lady wearing a Miss Haversham gown; draped grey over the buildings, old lace tattered round the edges.

In spring it should be lovely. Now those delicate trees in rue Magenta end their right-angled branches with dots of green. Tables spread out on terraces.

When I asked a friend how they do it – the French, this style – 'rigour' was the answer.

In August it feels walked upon. Parisians leave the city for the country, and in flow the tourists – in shorts! The city tries to hold up its head, tries to keep its edge, its style, through this indignity. We try not to slouch, but it's hard: we are hot and tired.

To me, London is a red city, a brick red city, and Paris is grey: a grey that changes. When it rains it's a dark grey, the pavements and umbrellas black.

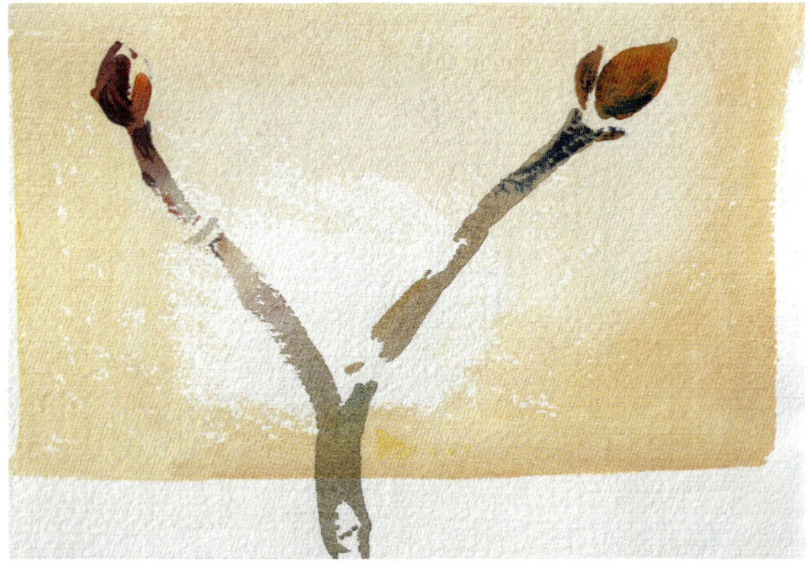

Buds, 2012, watercolour
6½ x 9 inches

Il pleure dans mon coeur
Comme il pleut sur la ville.

(There's weeping in my heart
When there's rain in the city.)
(Paul Verlaine, translated by William Rees)

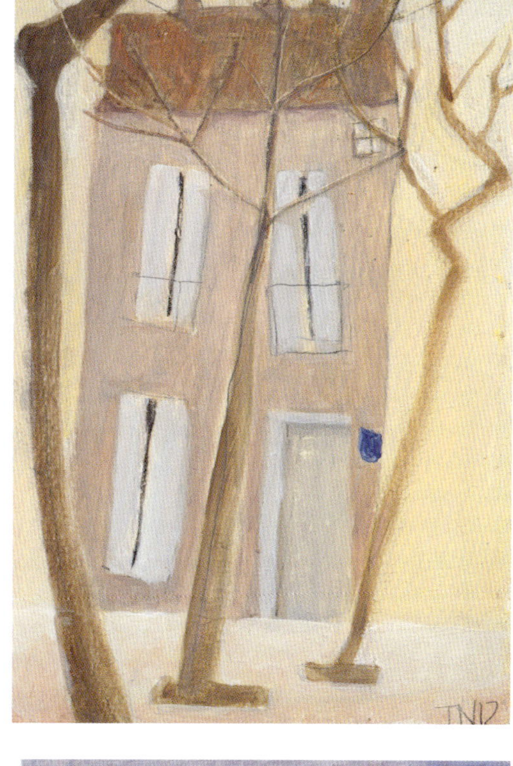

Paris between Trees, 2012, oil on board, 8 x 5 inches

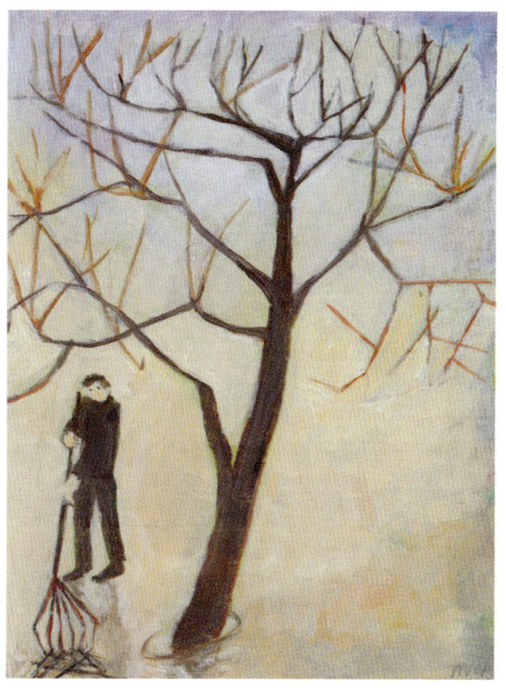

Raking, 2007, oil on board, 8 x 6 inches

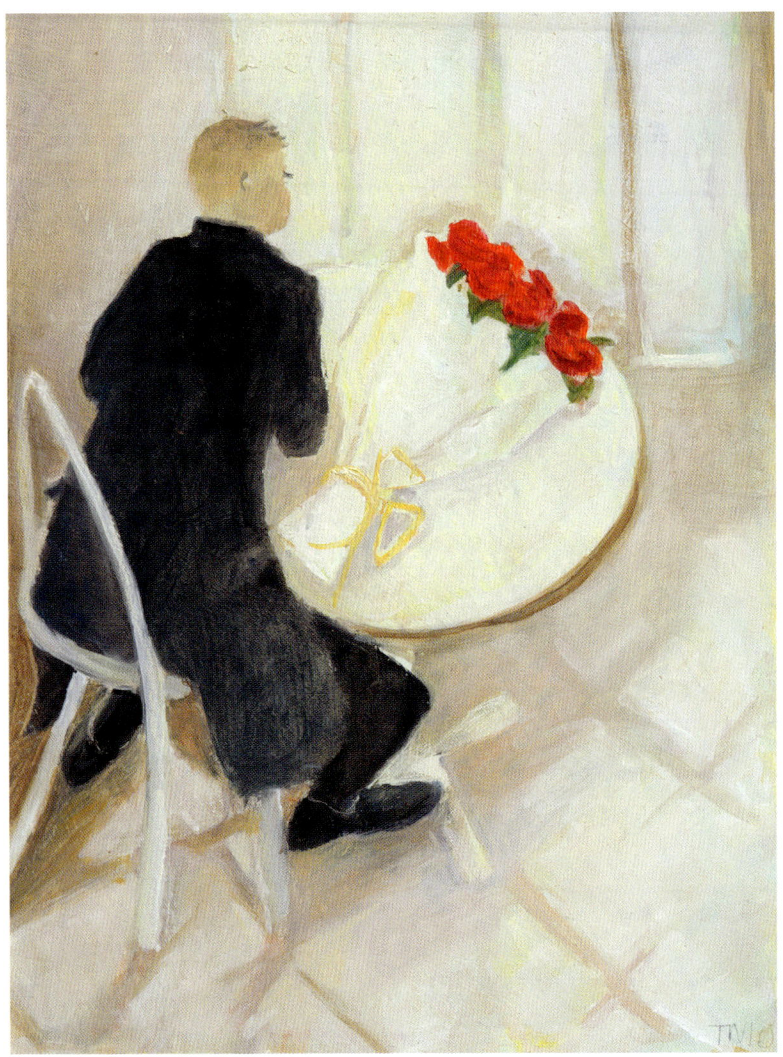

Anxious, 2010, oil on board, 9 x 6¾ inches

Morning Snow, 2007, oil on board, 7½ x 5 inches ➤

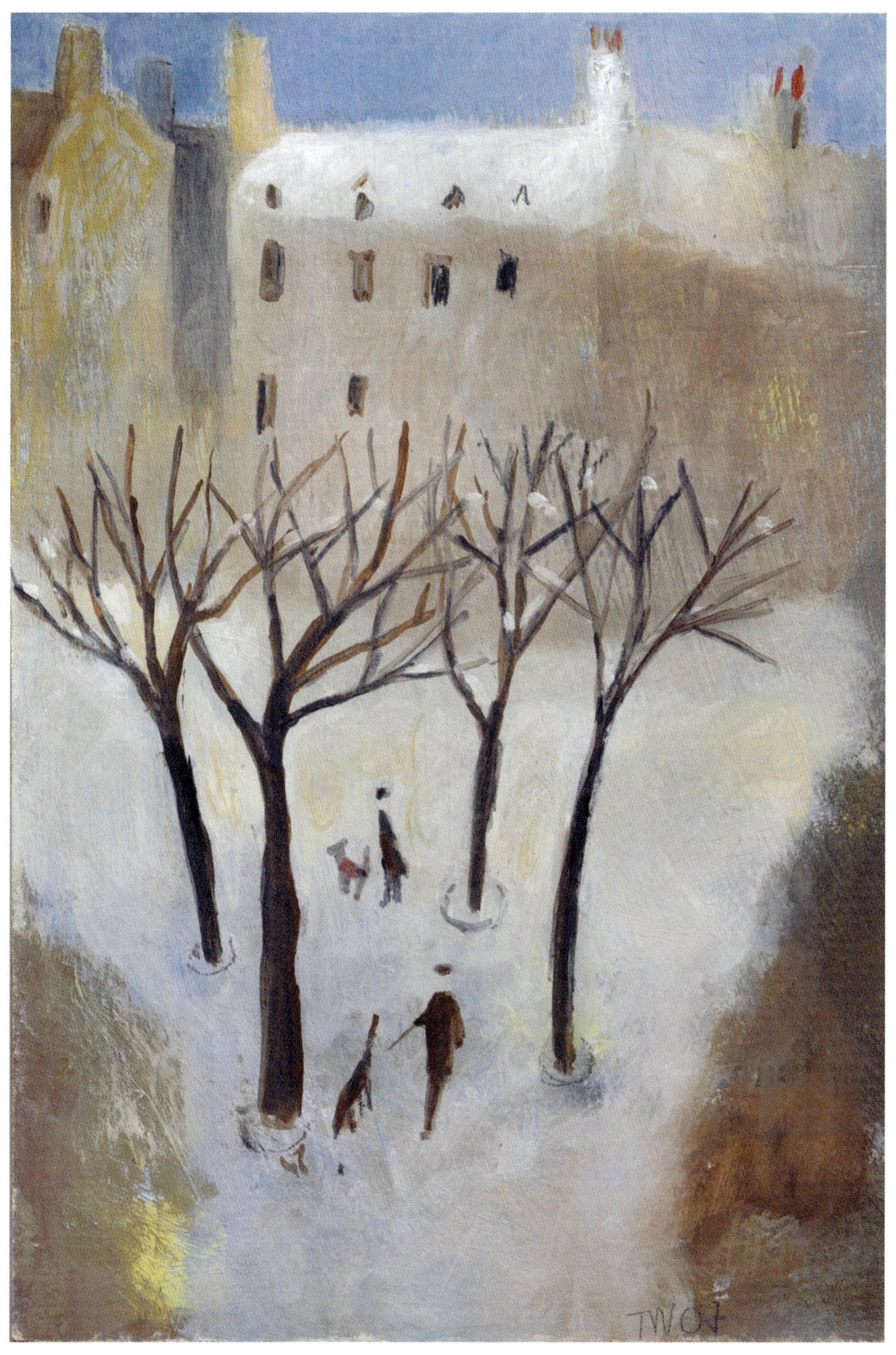

TW01

Like every visitor to Paris, I had made 'discoveries' that were known already to millions of people – the mysterious little attic room on the south face of Notre-Dame overlooking the Seine, or the crenel-lated brick tower that hides in a shrubbery near the western face of the Eiffel Tower... Then there were the discoveries that were purely archival – things that had vanished so completely that the imagina-tion had no purchase on the present: the unmarked location of the guillotine that beheaded Marie-Antoinette...

(from *Parisians: An Adventure History of Paris* by Graham Robb, 2010)

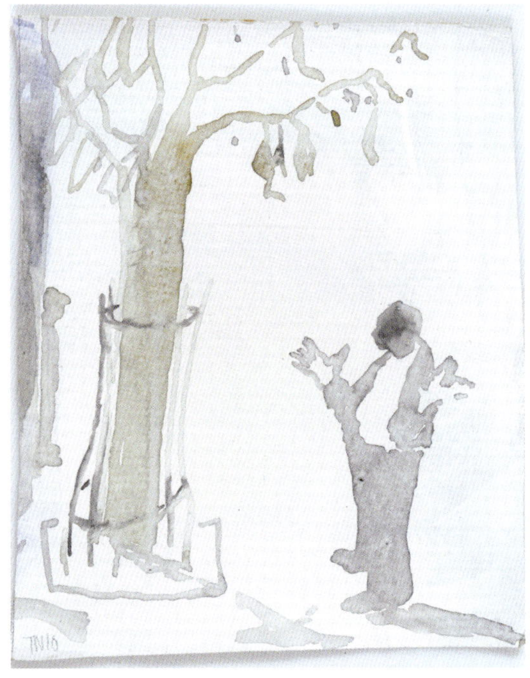

Talking, 2010, watercolour, 6 x 5 inches

CHAPTER I

Gold

Gold ring

We had just arrived and headed hesitantly towards Place Vendôme.
A man stopped us. He had found a gold ring. He said, 'I will give it to
the lady but you buy sandwich for me.' It was an old trick, but new to
us: a worthless ring, but what made it possible was that we were
outside a window of gold rings.

A cream limousine drew up outside a jeweller's in the Place Vendôme.
The chauffeur went round to let out a couple who went into the dark
interior of the shop towards the focus of their desire – a jewel.

The Glove Shop

In a heatwave in August an exclusive glove shop in the covered walk-
way was displaying its autumn collection. A single glove on a stand
stood to attention. Others lay elegantly – an exotic creature in cerulean
blue suede, a stout brown pair for a man to pull on, a gauntlet with a
tassel. They were behind bars, behind shadows and reflections of bars,
waiting in the gloomy light of the closed shop.

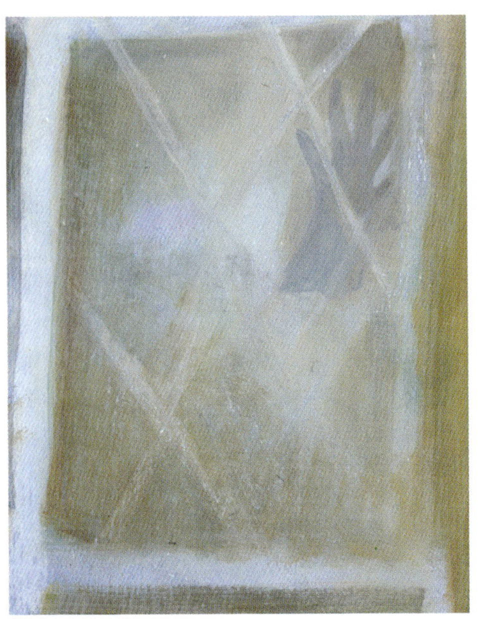

The Glove Shop, 2012, oil on board, 9 x 7 inches

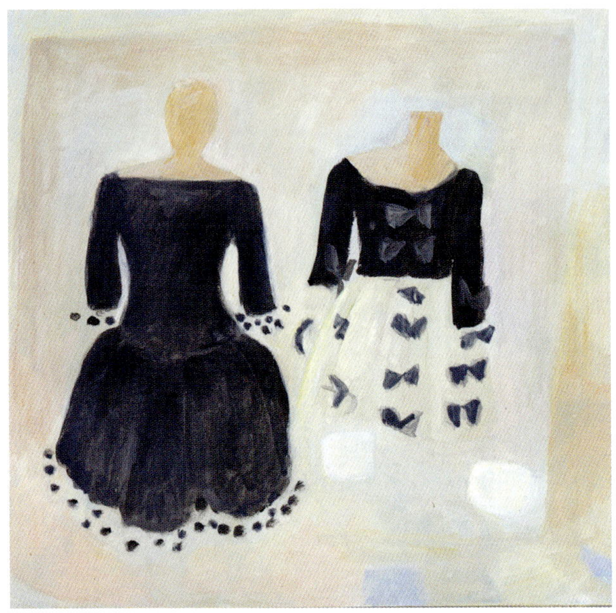

Dior and Chanel, 2012, oil on board, 8 x 9 inches

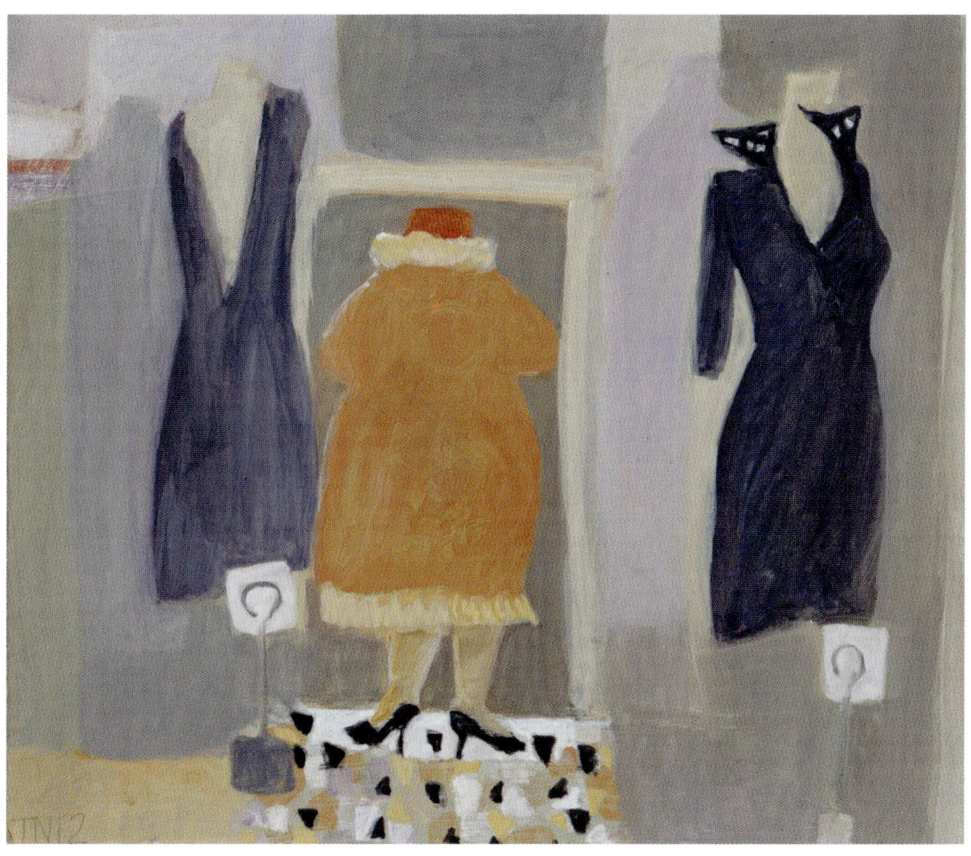

Learning Curve, 2010, oil on board, 5½ x 6½ inches

Camel is very popular, camels in lots of shades.

Dress shabbily, they remember the dress; dress impeccably, they remember the woman. Coco Chanel

And in the interior of La Crème – so many brides' dresses, so many weddings.

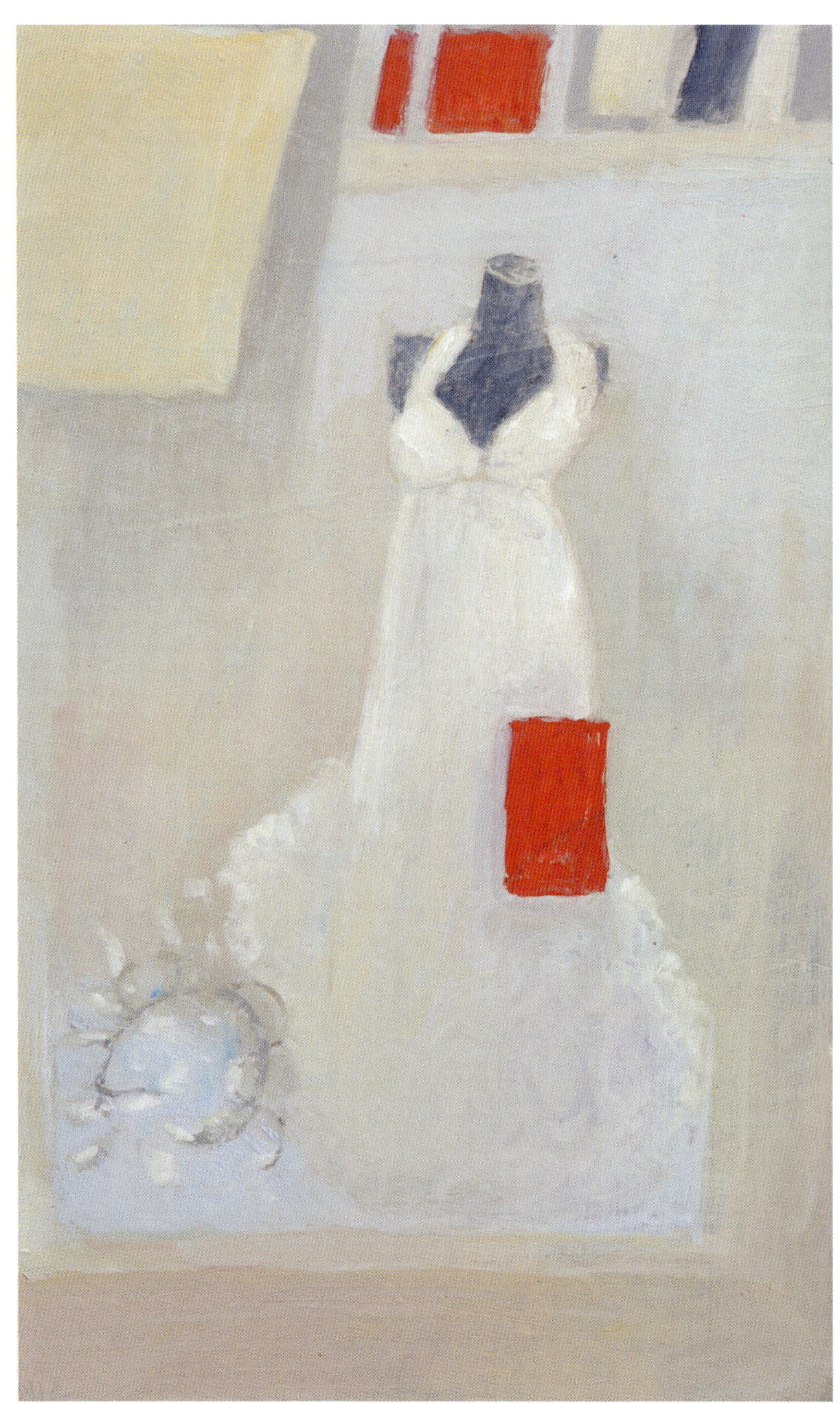

La Crème, 2012, oil on board
(double-page spread)
part one: 9 x 5¼ inches;
part two: 9 x 7¼

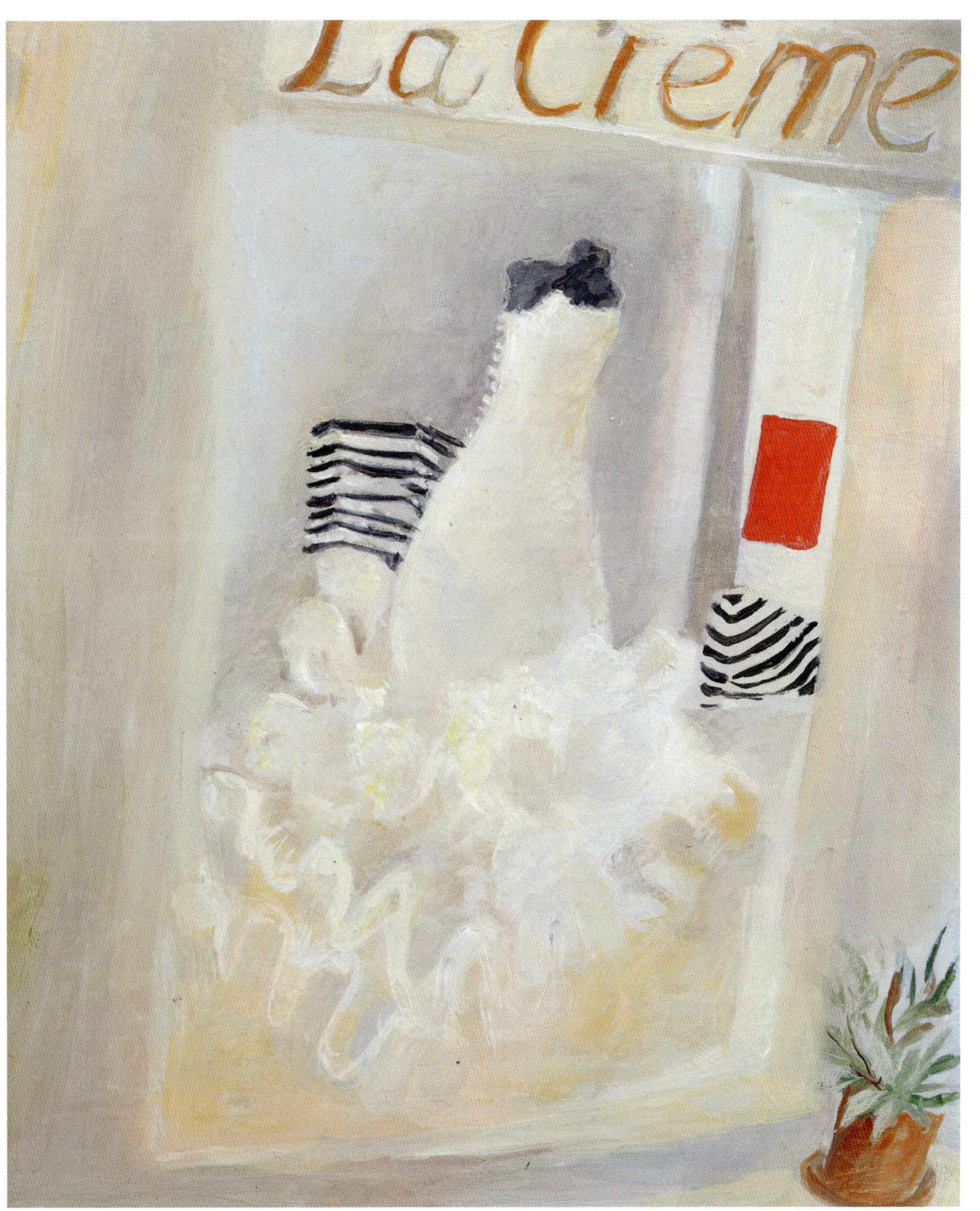
La Crème

Arcades

Narrow covered walkways, early shopping
malls. Those which have not been
modernised remain as they were: dusky
backwaters lined with shops bathed in a
green light filtering in from the glass roof:
'human aquariums', Aragon calls them.

In his *Paris Peasant*, 1926, he describes
how people appear out of the gloom 'in
sunless corridors' with 'a glaucous gleam,
seemingly filtered through deep water, with
the special quality of pale brilliance of a leg
suddenly revealed under a lifted skirt.'

The shops are usually small, dark and
interesting – books, prints, outside and in.
At the back, a piled table and a small metal
staircase spiralling to mysterious upstairs
rooms, net-curtained against prying
pigeons.

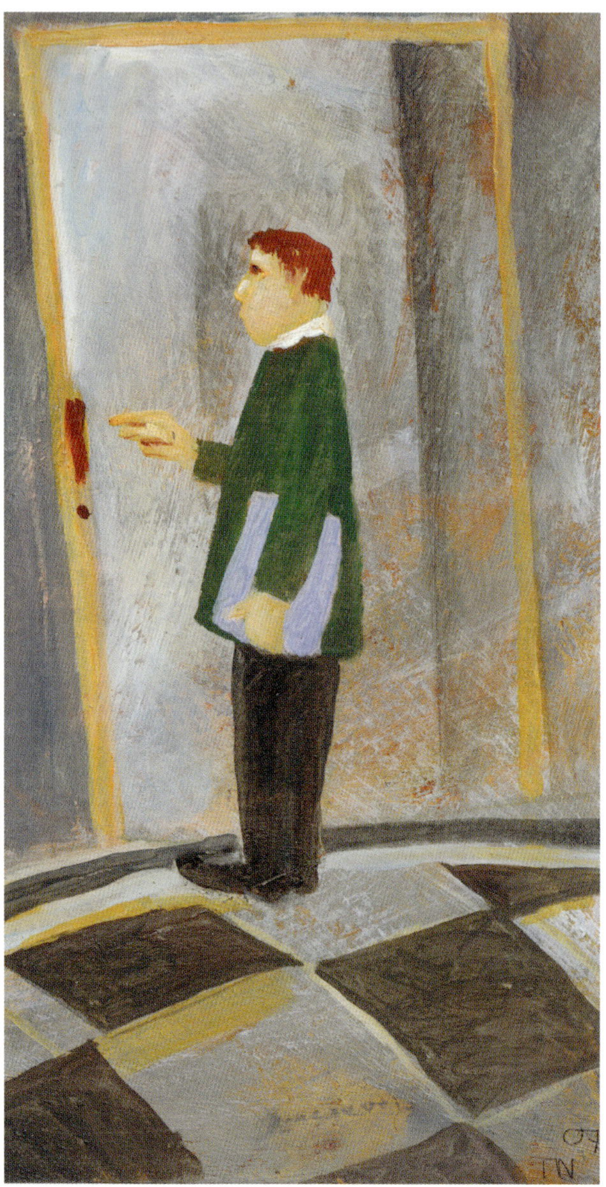

Some Men Can't Resist Buying Books, 2007, oil on board, 7¾ x 4 inches

The shops can be small, so can the things they sell. There's one with peculiar toys: tiny dolls perch on wine glasses, watched over by an assistant perched on a stool. One window is very full of miniature china dogs. Another shop is devoted to dolls' houses, which need tiny vegetables, little mats and tasteful wallpaper. Then there's a stamp shop where a woman, not so small, is delicately sorting stamps, mounting them in a big blue book.

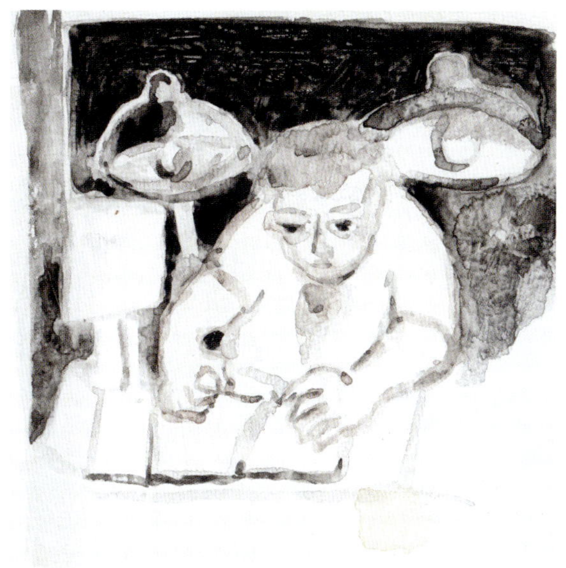

Stamping, 2012, watercolour, 7 x 7 inches

Little things held with tweezers.

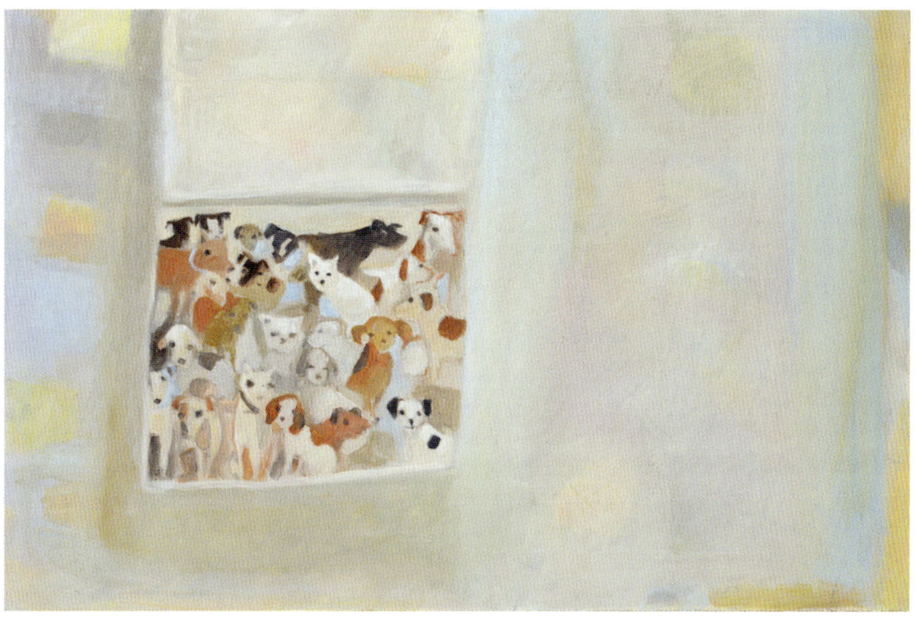

Tiny Dog Shop, 2012, oil on board, 6¼ x 10½ inches

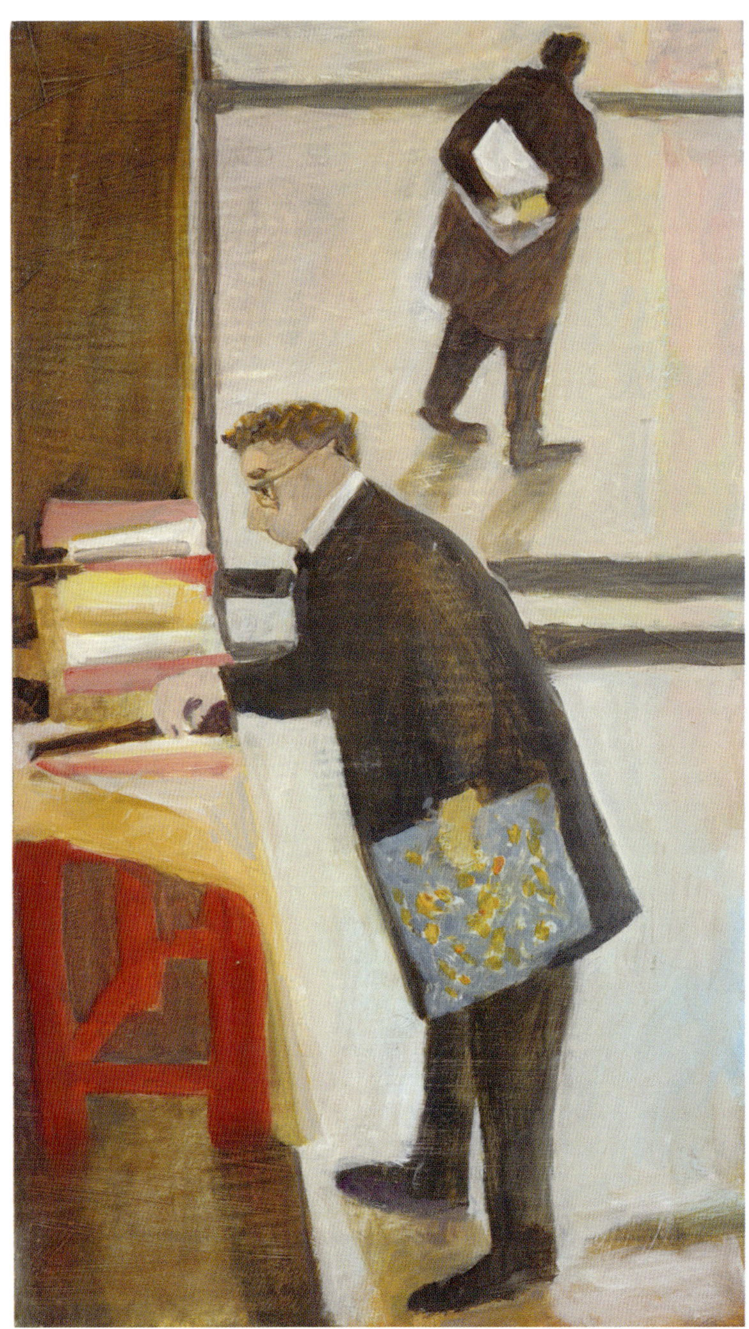

Books, 2007, oil on board, 10½ x 6 inches

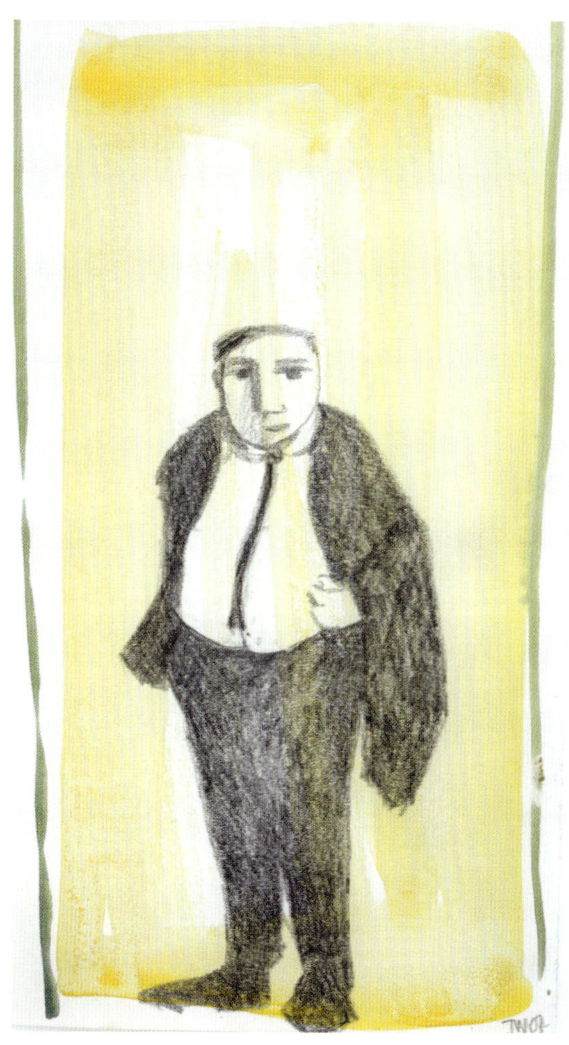

Man Interested, 2007, watercolour, 8¼ x 4½ inches

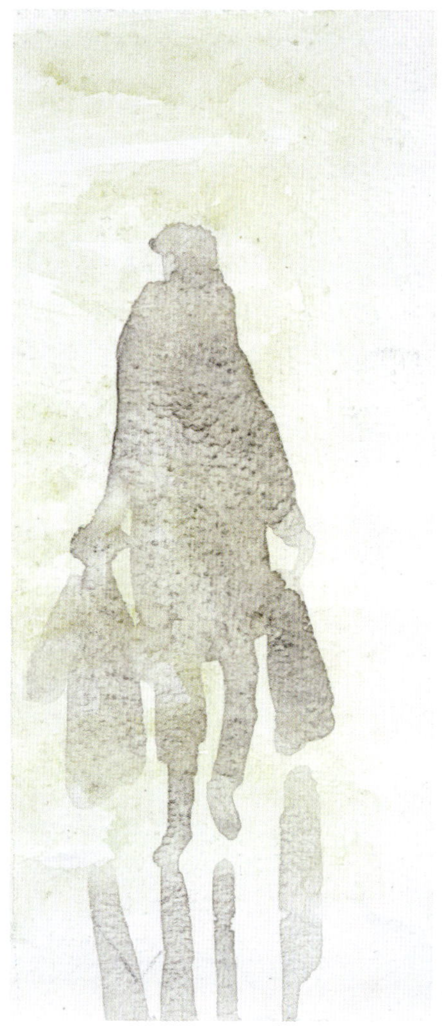

Feeling Faint, 2012, watercolour, 7½ x 3¼ inches

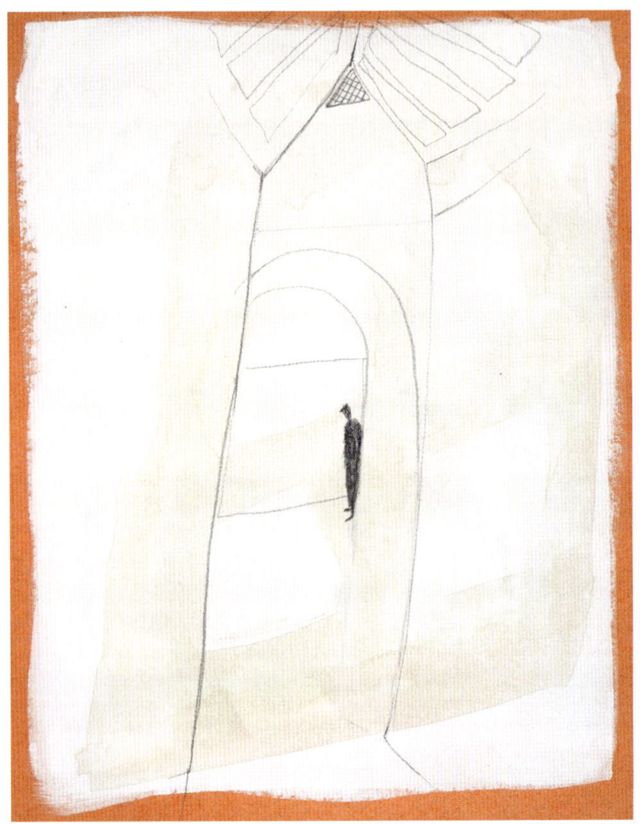

Out, 2012, pencil and watercolour, 10 x 8 inches

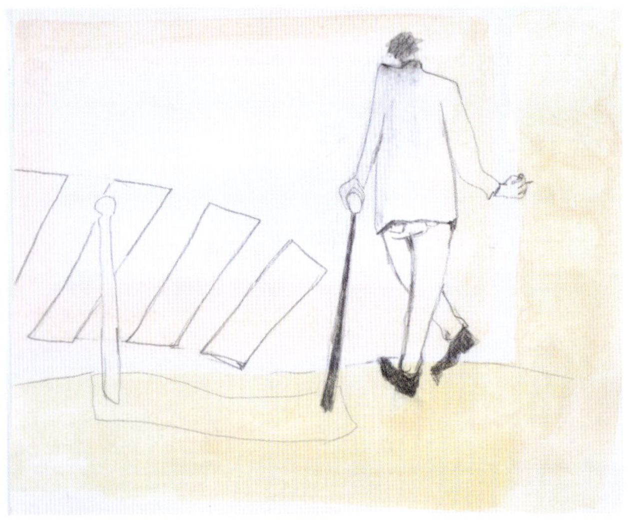

A Wait, 2012, pencil and watercolour, 5½ x 6¼ inches

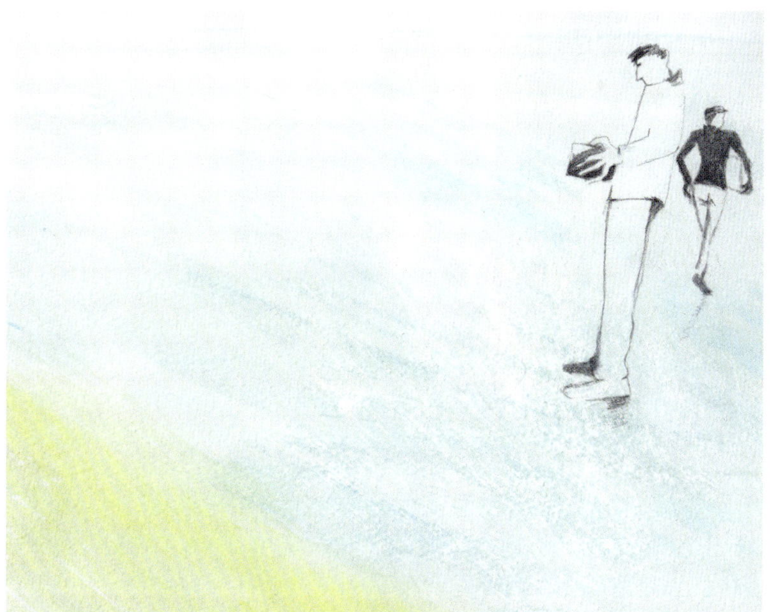

The Cut of the Coat, 2012
pencil and watercolour, 9 x 11½ inches

Shops that have more style
than things in them

*In the 60s, I used to stay in a hotel on the rue de Seine, which I
shared with a lorry driver during the day. This meant that the bed
was made up twice a day. The only thing that reminded me that I
shared a bed was the smell of stale breath when I came in.*
Telfer Stokes

*When, aged 14, I found myself on the loose in Paris, I set out to track
down copies of Paris-Hollywood, a large-format magazine of tinted
erotic photos of women in lingerie, of which I had once found copies
at a news stall in London. Having failed to find copies on public sale,
I made my way to the publishers' address, just off the Champs
Elysées, and, feeling that I was doing something very dangerous,
found my way up to the office. A large panelled room with a man
and a secretary, nothing exciting. I exaggerated my age, but they were
unconvinced by me, so I left empty-handed. Laws against selling such
publications to persons under 18 were strictly enforced in those days.*
Bob Jackson

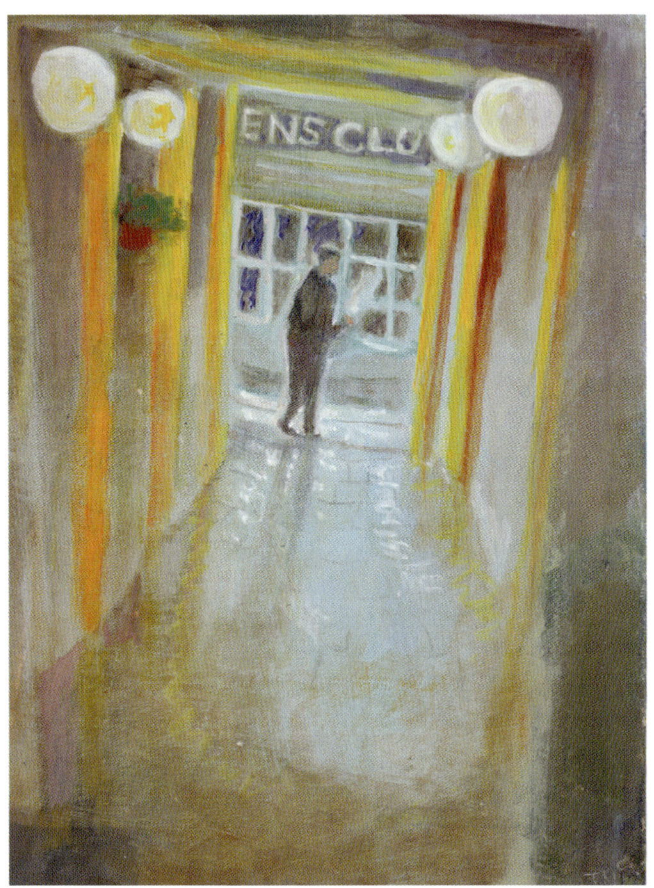

Men's Club, 2012, oil on board, 9 x 6¾ inches

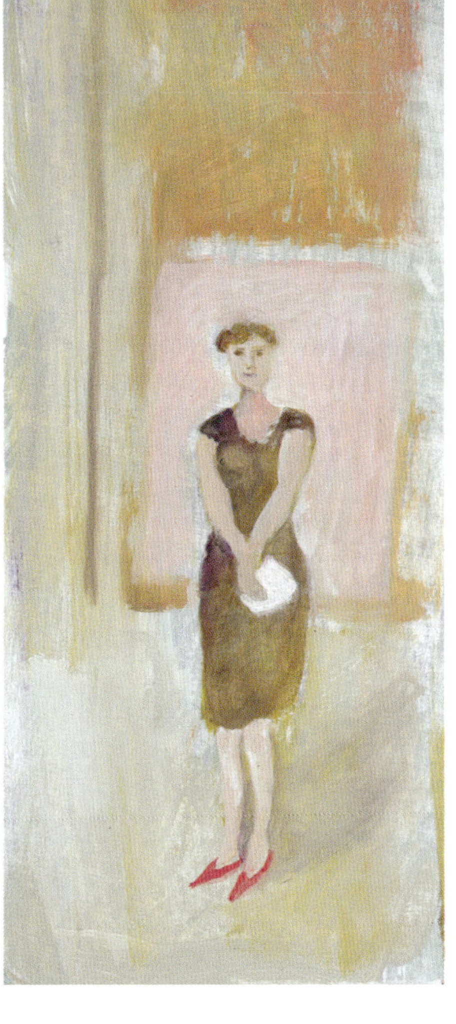

Value, 2010, oil on card, 7¾ x 3½ inches

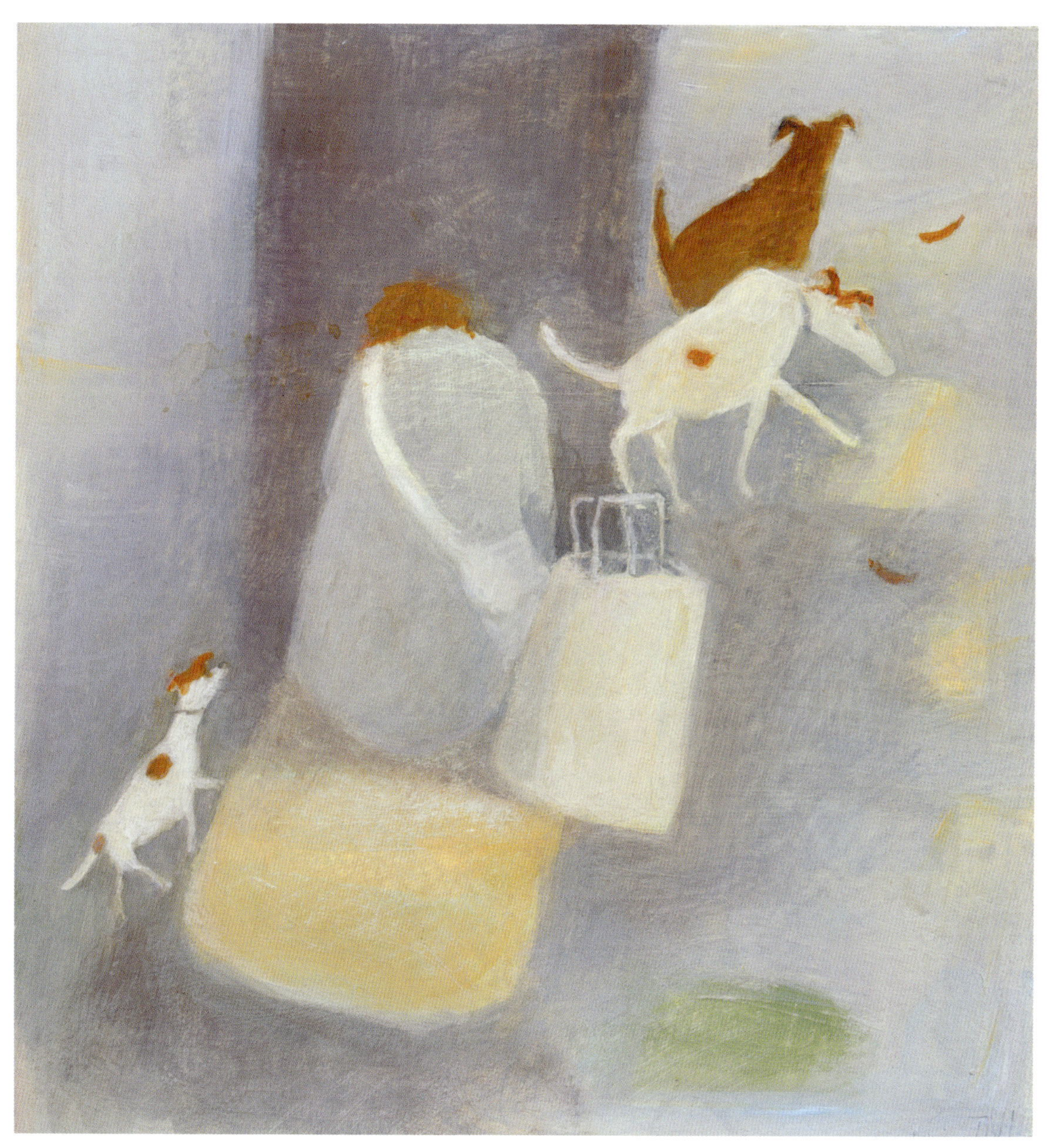

Saturday Lunchtime, 2012, oil on card, 9¾ x 9 inches

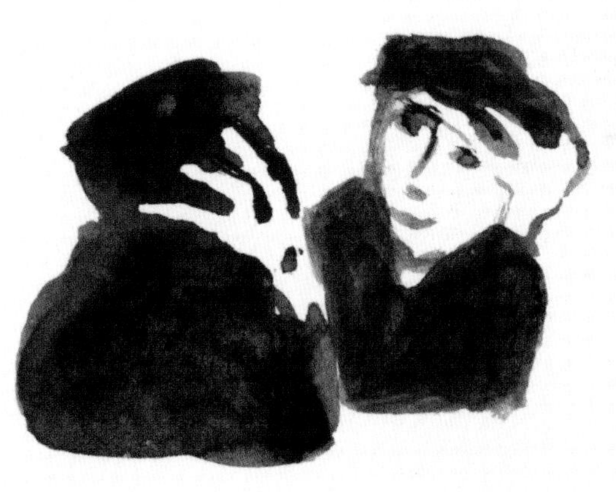

Talk Talk, 2012, watercolour, 4 x 6 inches

CHAPTER 2

Glass

Glass, glasses, windows and mirrors – to reflect the outside in and the inside out. They are in the entrances, up the stairs, behind the bar, even behind the pastries. Often at the side of a shop window there's a slither of you. There are hundreds of you in Paris.

The glazed pastries. One can only eat one. When I draw them, I eat them with my eyes.

I'm not a great foodie person but my partner is, so I've been to the 'best' restaurants. It's the tablecloths that impress me – all that ironing! The napkins so thick they don't fold well.

The American group sat down and so did we. We talked of America and England, not taking in that this place specialised in fine wines and food from the Burgundy region. A beer's a beer anywhere.

This one? Fifteen hundred francs. See, it's signed and dated...

*the hemispheric paperweight of thick glass... evokes the bottom of the sea,
a garden à la française, a jar of Viennese acid-drops, and costs fifteen
hundred francs...*

*In the days when my very dear Annie de Pène and I used to haunt flea-
markets, we paid three francs, or a hundred sous, for these playthings so
sanctified and revalued by fashion... Annie had a thing about a paperweight where imprisoned air bubbles shone like globules of mercury above
a drowned pansy.*

(from 'Paperweights', an essay by Colette, c.1925)

Patisserie, 2012, oil on board, 10 x 8¾ inches

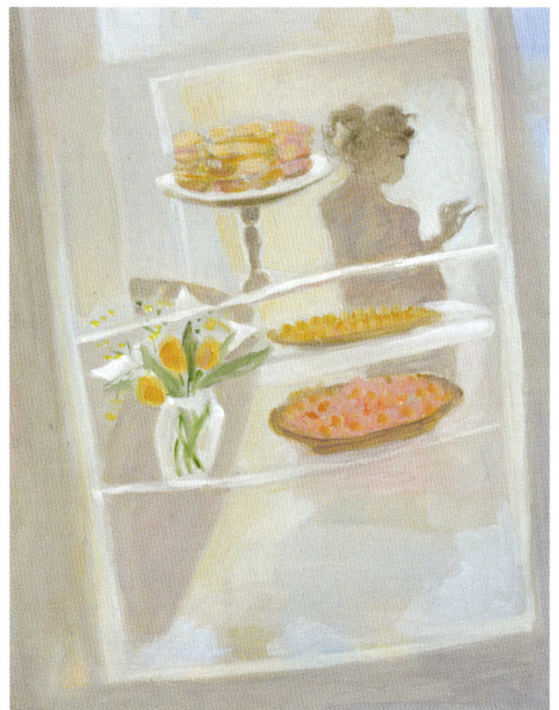

The Dainty Eater, 2009, oil on card, 9 x 6¾ inches

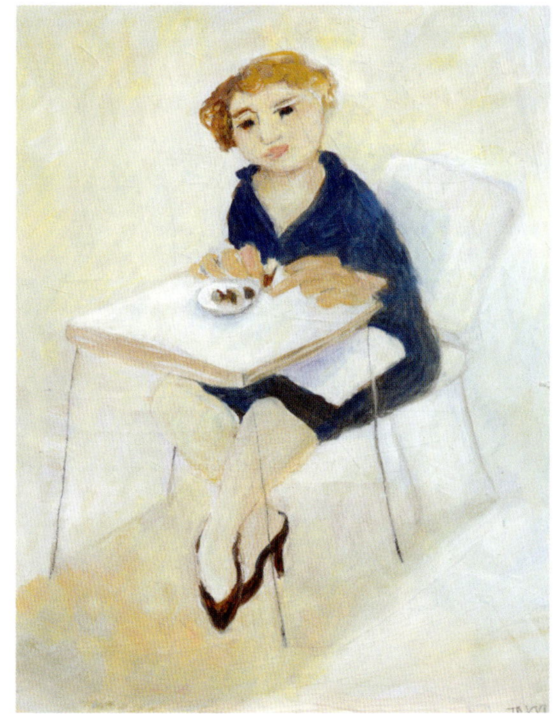

In the patisserie

Macaroons like medals and the tarts – like tarts.

This café had violent orange, red and yellow plastic chairs and cups
to match. Wonderful against the grey of the streets. Two exquisite
girls took their coffee outside and smoked. A large man, perched
on a stool, went through his paper at the counter. The barman
returned, his arms full of baguettes. The coffee machine let out
steam like a small engine. Saucers were slapped down. It felt active
and purposeful.

Cafés with little blankets for your knees, a nice touch.

If She Comes In, It Will Change Everything, 2012, oil on board, 8¼ x 9 inches

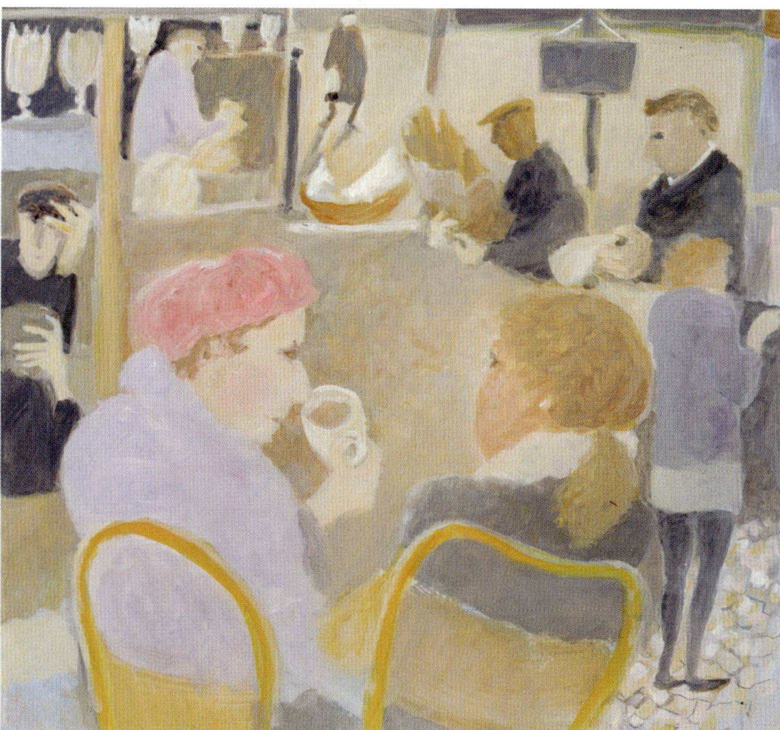

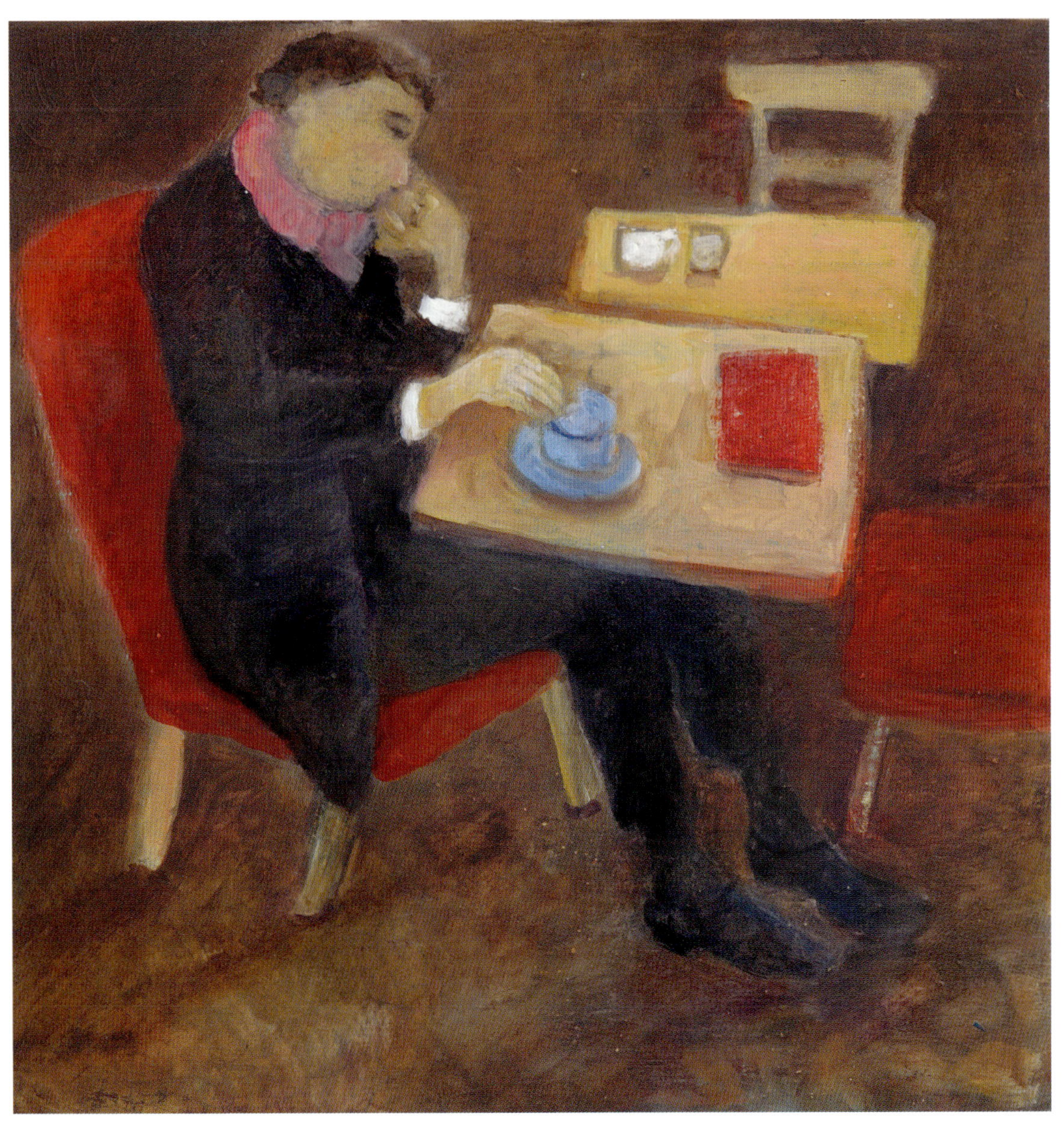

The Frenchman, 2007, oil on board, 8¼ x 8 inches

At ease with pleasure

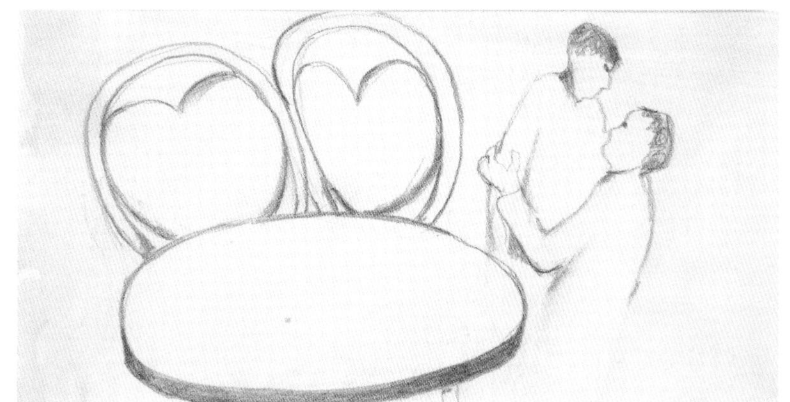

Needing a Chair, 2012,
pencil and watercolour
3 x 6 inches

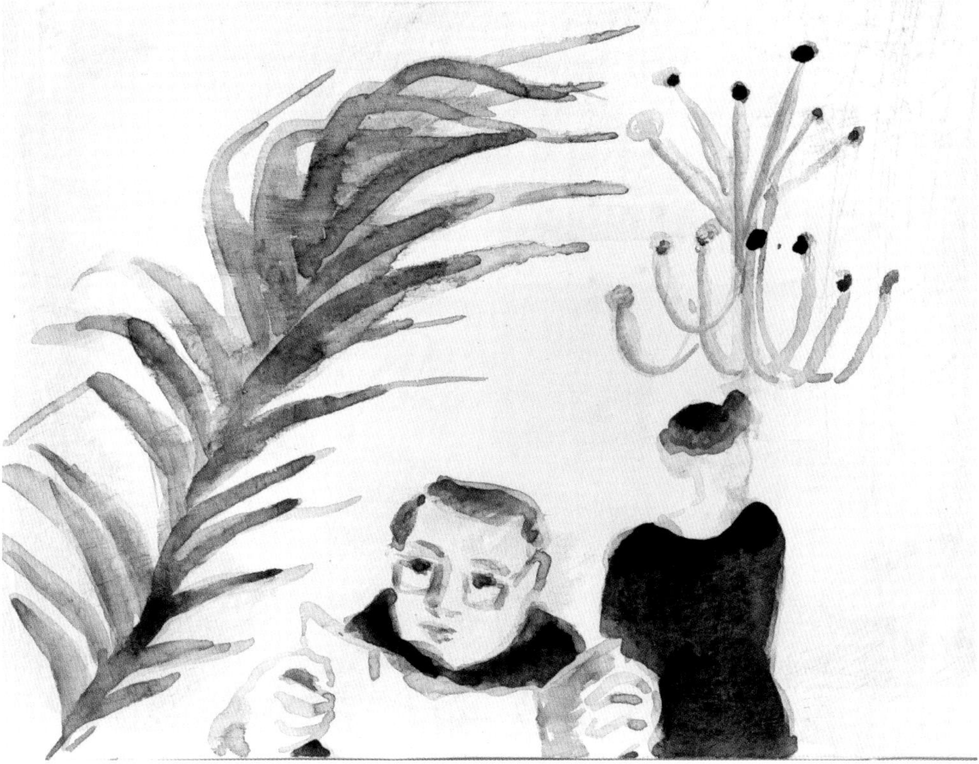

Smart Place, 2012, watercolour, 7 x 9 inches

The eater

At a Sicilian café with red checked tablecloths at a late lunch hour, a single man
exchanged a few words with the proprietor,
polished off a good dish of pasta and cleaned
his bowl with bread. Only then he reached
for his tumbler of red wine. Coffee and
crumbs. He dabbed his moustache, rolled his
napkin into a ball and looked around.

Studying the menu with a gold ring on his
little finger.

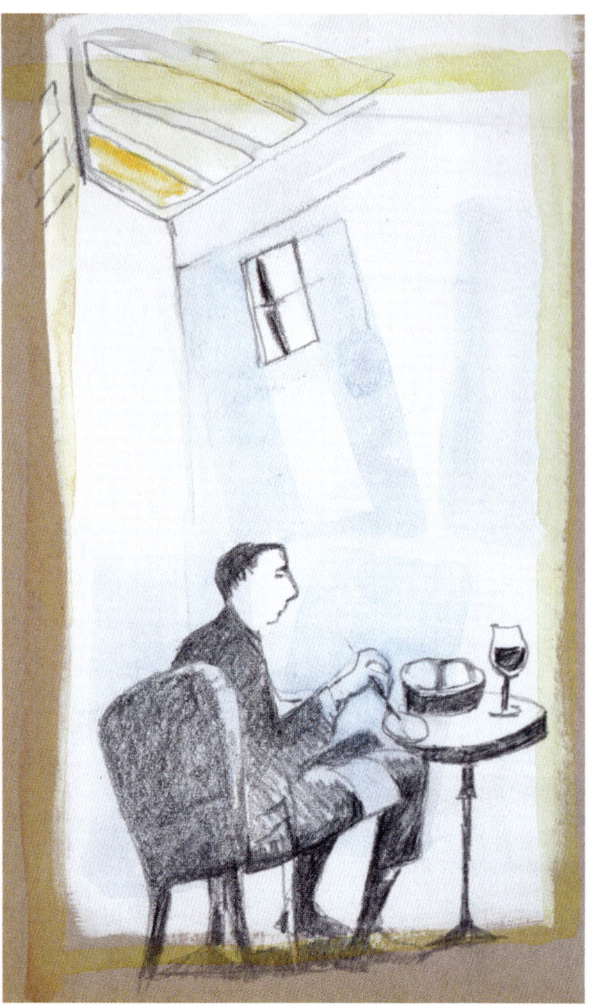

Twiddling, 2012, pencil and watercolour, 8 x 5 inches

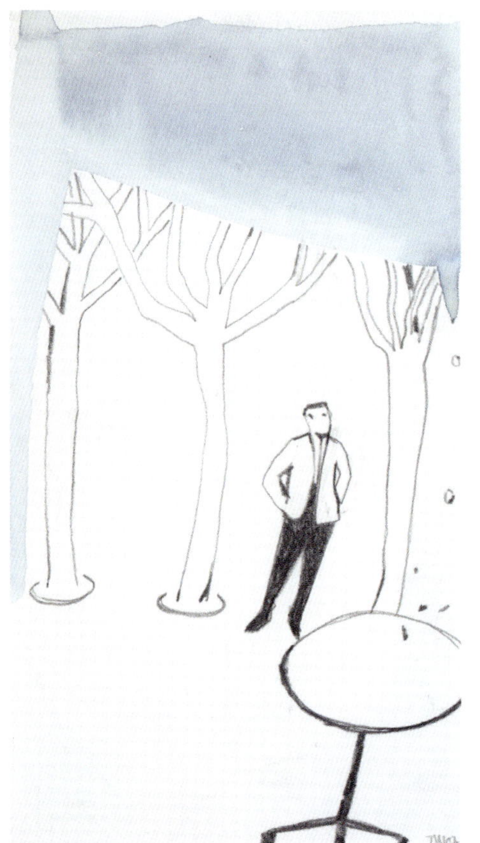

Wishful, 2007, pencil and watercolour, 8¼ x 4¾ inches

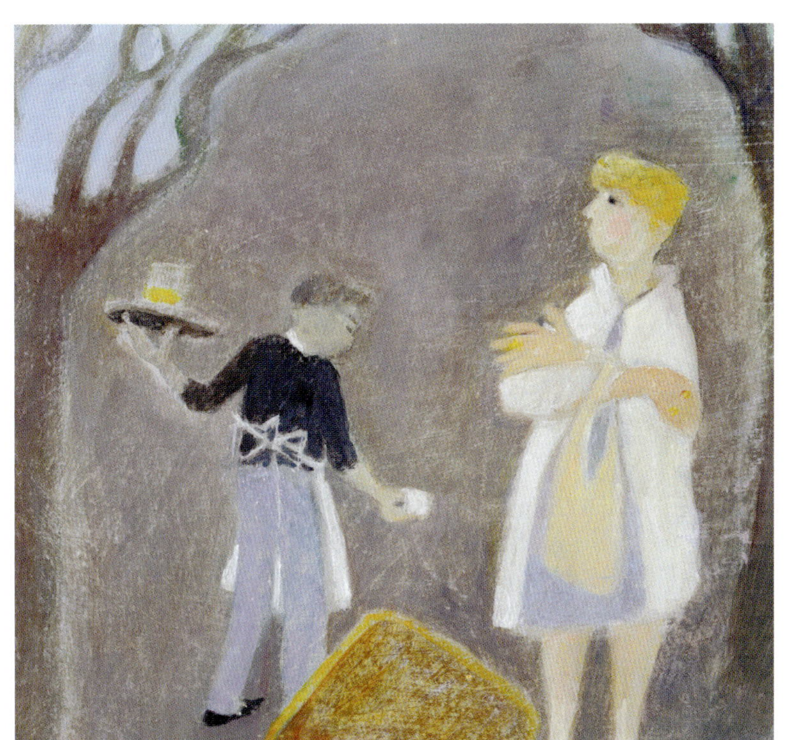

Street Life, 2012
oil on board
8 x 10 inches

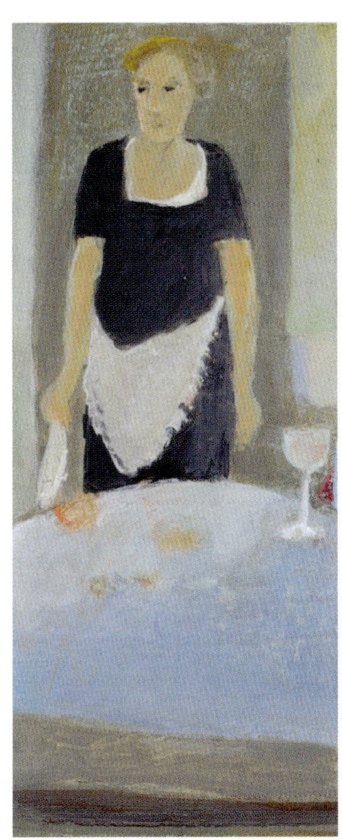

Waitress, 2012, oil on board, 6 x 2½ inches

The sun crept across the café tables
like a crazy devil out to get you. The
blinds were lowered on both sides.
We were huddled together in the
shade.

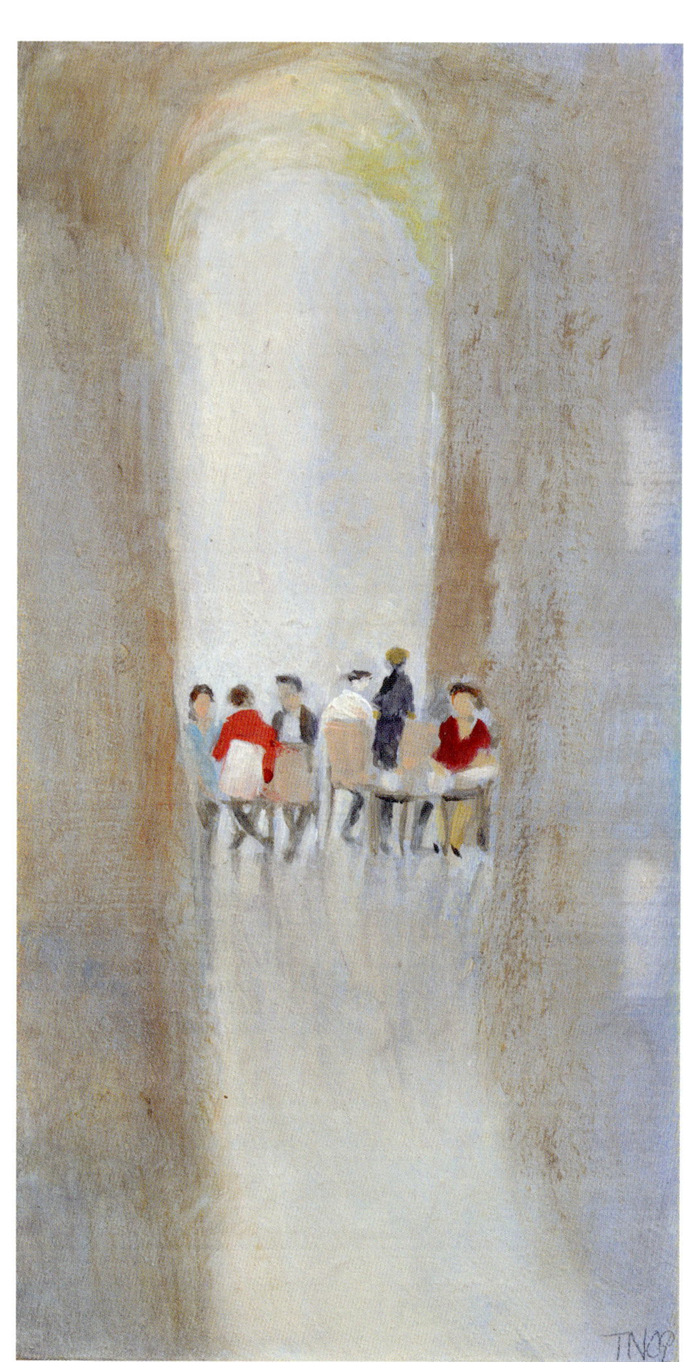

Busy with the Sunday Papers, 2009
oil on board, 8 x 4 inches

Hot and Cold

We crossed an open bit by the Panthéon. It was sleeting, slobs of wet, minus 5°C, February. My lover of then was being beastly. Tears stopped me from eating whatever it was – expensive in a skillet. The patron plonked a cognac down – on the house. But what I remember most was the loo – it was so small. A little cupboard at the turn of the stairs.

February and March have poured on Paris the blackest rain that ever fell from a grey sky, snow the colder because it melts, hail crackling underfoot like a broken necklace... taxi-drivers run for the nearest bar, delivery boys under open porches turn into statues of polished oilskin... You can see the Place de l'Opéra, the boulevard and the rue de la Paix deserted, gleaming, bombarded by the wrath from on high...

(from 'Journey for Myself', an essay by Colette, c.1925)

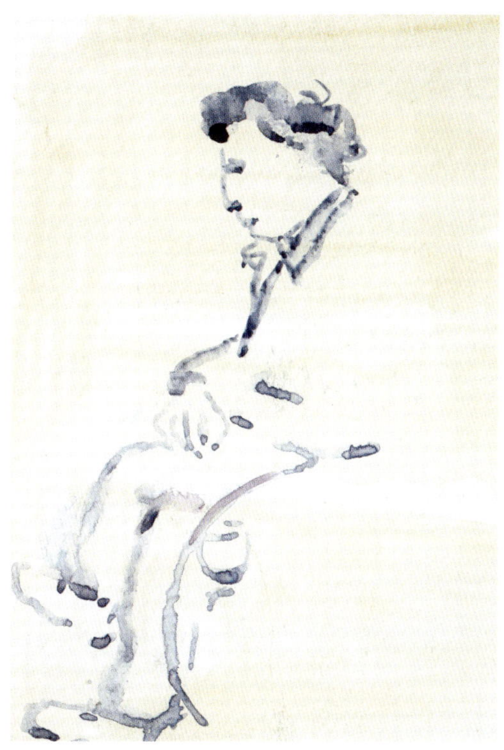

On the Terrace, 2012, watercolour, 8¾ x 6 inches

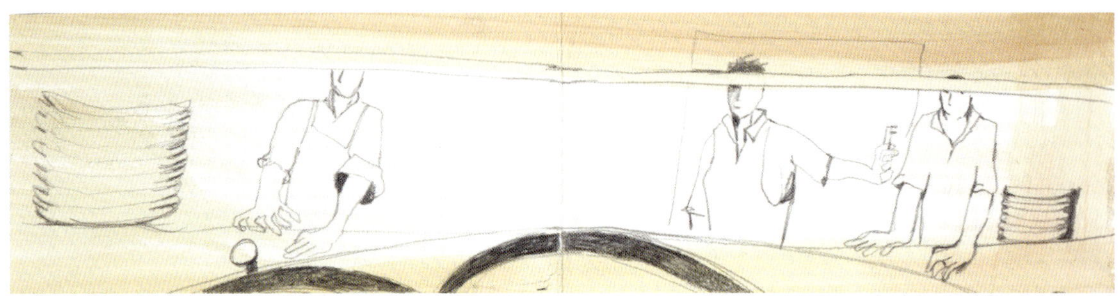

Behind the Scenes, 2012, pencil and watercolour,
3½ x 13¼ inches

In the middle of an August afternoon a fat man went into an empty
restaurant and ordered himself the biggest ice cream sundae. As he ate
he kept looking around as if expecting his wife to appear and scold him.

A good French restaurant has those real net curtains that run, loopy
loop, along a rail at eye level, a brown interior, and rabbit on the menu.

Hope Mirrlees writes of looking down from the top floor of an old hotel:

> *I gaze down at the narrow rue de Beaune.*
> *Hawkers chant their wares liturgically*
>
> ....
> *Workmen in pale blue:*
> *Barrows of vegetables:*
> *Busy dogs:*
> *They come and go.*
> *They are very small.*
>
> ....
> *Little funny things ceaselessly happening.*
> (from Hope Mirrlees: 'Paris, A Poem', 1919)

CHAPTER 3

Markets

The sun is rising.
Soon les Halles will open,
The sky is saffron behind the two towers of Nôtre-Dame.
(From Hope Mirrlees, 'Paris, A Poem', 1919)

Flowers seem to be necessary for Parisians who often live in small apartments, without gardens. Men don't look embarrassed to be seen carrying very stylish bouquets.

As I approached one stall, at first I thought the flowers on display looked so sad – battered by the elements. Then I realised that rose petals had been artfully scattered on the pavements beneath – to create a charming effect.

The Arrangement

Monday morning rain. That greyness that turns stone black. A cheap flower stall, its bunches wrapped in triangles of bright papers are set out in rows of grey pots. Itself an arrangement. A sudden breeze – as if turned on from a wind machine – blows green leaves down from the trees all over them.

Tightly bunched flower shop. It was mostly on the outside. Inside it was cool and gloomy. I hardly noticed the man, who was wearing a camou-flage jacket.

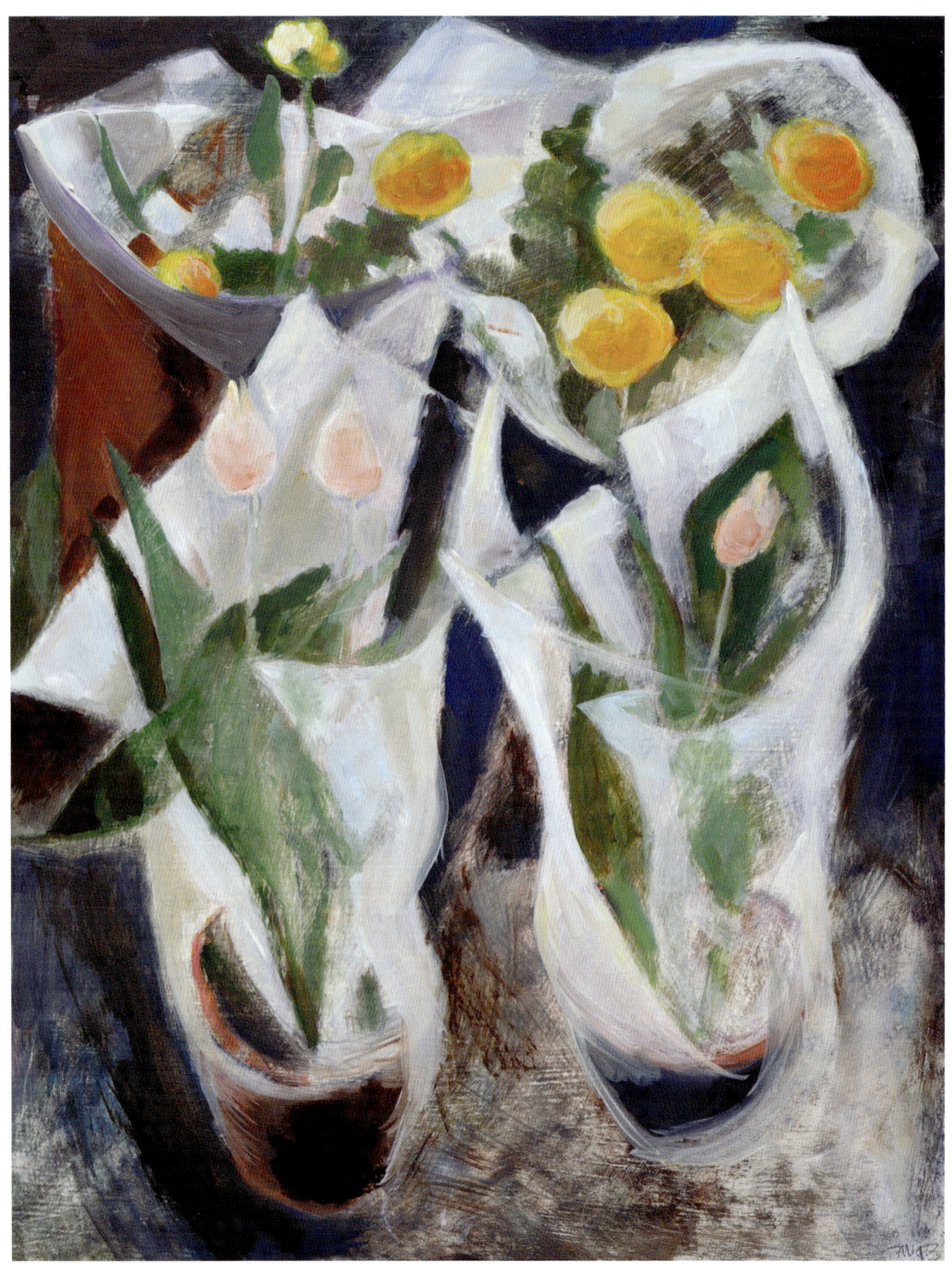

Wrapped Flowers, 2013, oil on board, 24 x 18 inches

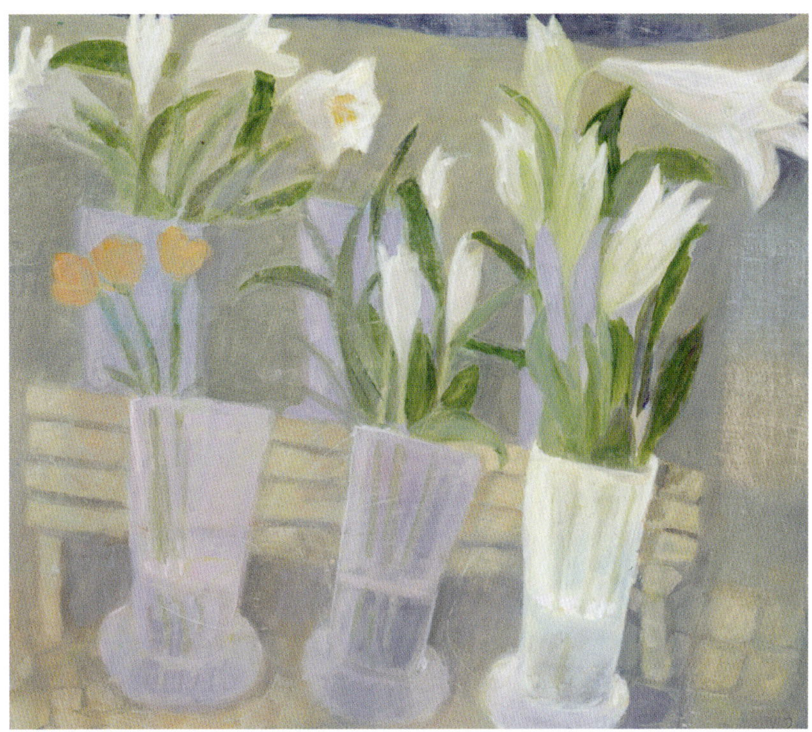

Lilies Say a Lot, 2012
oil on board, 9 x 10 inches

Lilies on a damp day.
Their pots were violet, lilac and pink

An open doorway, in a seemingly no-account street, one day revealed to me a kind of deep provincial paradise, adorned with ancient weeping ash-trees, magnolias, stone vases, sleeping cats, and even apple-trees in cordons, planted in palisade around the lawn...

O you bucolic Parisians, decked in May with lilies of the valley, gatherers of lilac, you go into ecstasies over a tuft of grass or a snowdrop, aren't you the guardians of Paris's remaining rural secrets?

(from 'Captive Gardens', an essay by Colette, c.1925)

A man with flowers and a woman without.

The hotel lobby is full of the smell of lilies. Do these green buds open slowly or with a pop for the night porter?

Her long white fingers separated the lilies.

Fruit and vegetables

Very good-looking men and small older ladies are buying vegetables. The
woman needs a lettuce. You buy one very good lettuce and it's a perform-
ance. The stallholder flips through till he finds the one, which he holds up
triumphantly. She nods. It goes into the bag. Her dog has to straddle the
stream of water flowing along the kerb. Then fruits need to be purchased.
She's done well. Now the purse can be snapped shut and she can move on.
All without taking off her fine leather gloves.

Lychees and boots with pom-poms.

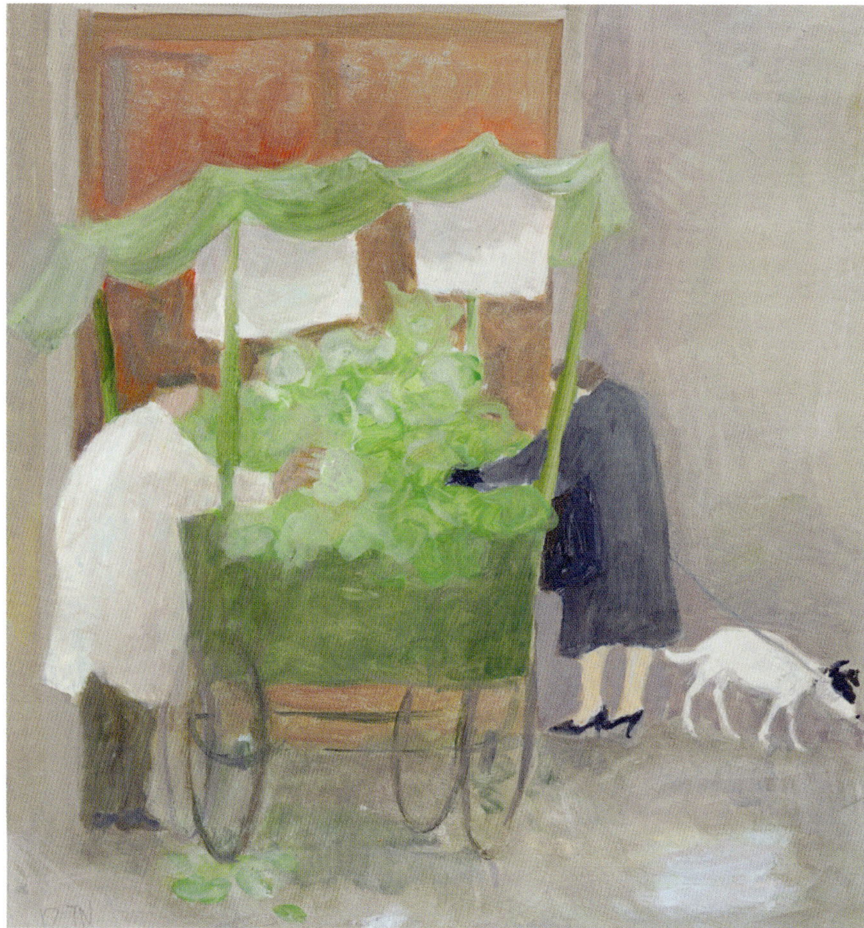

Lettuces, 2012
oil on card
7¾ x 7 inches

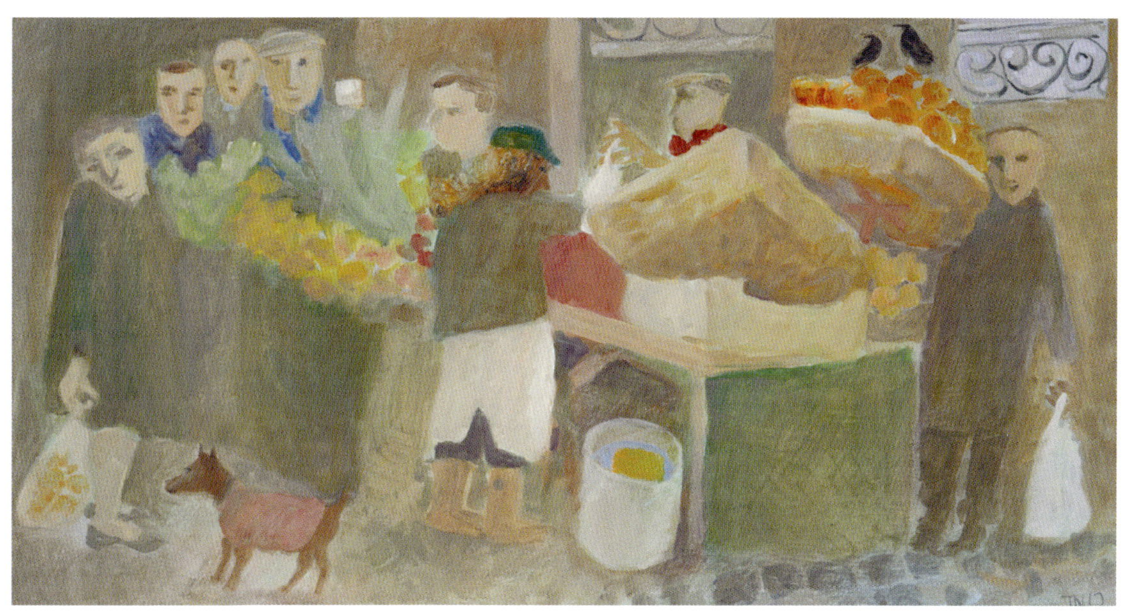

Marketing, 2012
oil on board
8 x 14½ inches

We sit outside a café on the street between two stalls selling mush-rooms, and eat mushrooms. These are small, black and buttered, flavoured with garlic and parsley. Very good with a beer on Saturday after shopping.

We went from bar to bar, the meanest, lowest, most dismal ones, where Bob loved the atmosphere and where he was fond of listening to the people chatting at the counter, workmen in overalls, little shopkeepers from the neighbourhood, who came in for a quickie. We took most of our meals in those simple little restaurants, where the bill of fare is written on a slate and where the smell of fried onions always hangs in the air.

(from *Le grand Bob*, 1954, by Georges Simenon)

Cheeses

The stall seems to have a piece of terrain from every region of France, and just as various: cheeses in texture like chalk, limestone and granite. Mild goat's cheese sits on clean straw, a feta-type lies under scummy water and cone-shaped bombs of strong Boulette d'Avesnes are coated with gold paprika. The butter is neatly patted, and yoghurt ladled from nice brown jars.

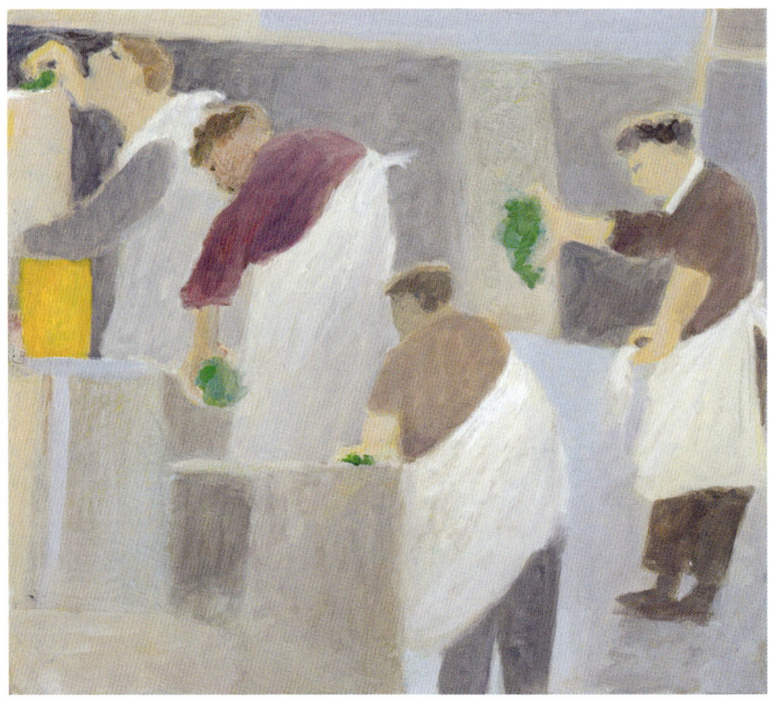

Cheese, 2012, oil on card, 6½ x 11

Butchers Cleaning Up, 2012
oil on board, 6¾ x 7¼ inches

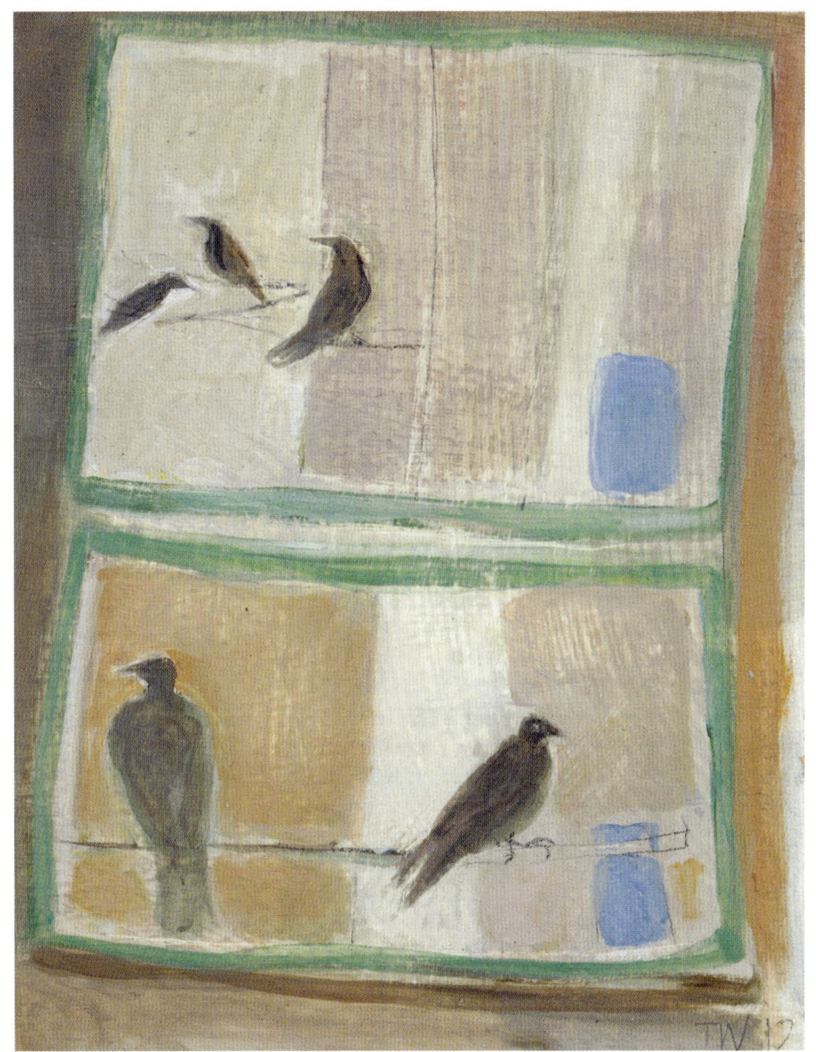

Birds, 2012
oil on board
5¼ x 4 inches

The Bird Market

The bird market appears on Sundays. It features little birds in little cages, expensive dog accessories and millet, which come in different colours. Scattered underneath the cages is a pattern of millet husks. In one cage I thought the birds looked particularly alert – then I realised that they were bald. You can have cages and birds in a range of colours. Lots of cages hang from the ceiling without birds.

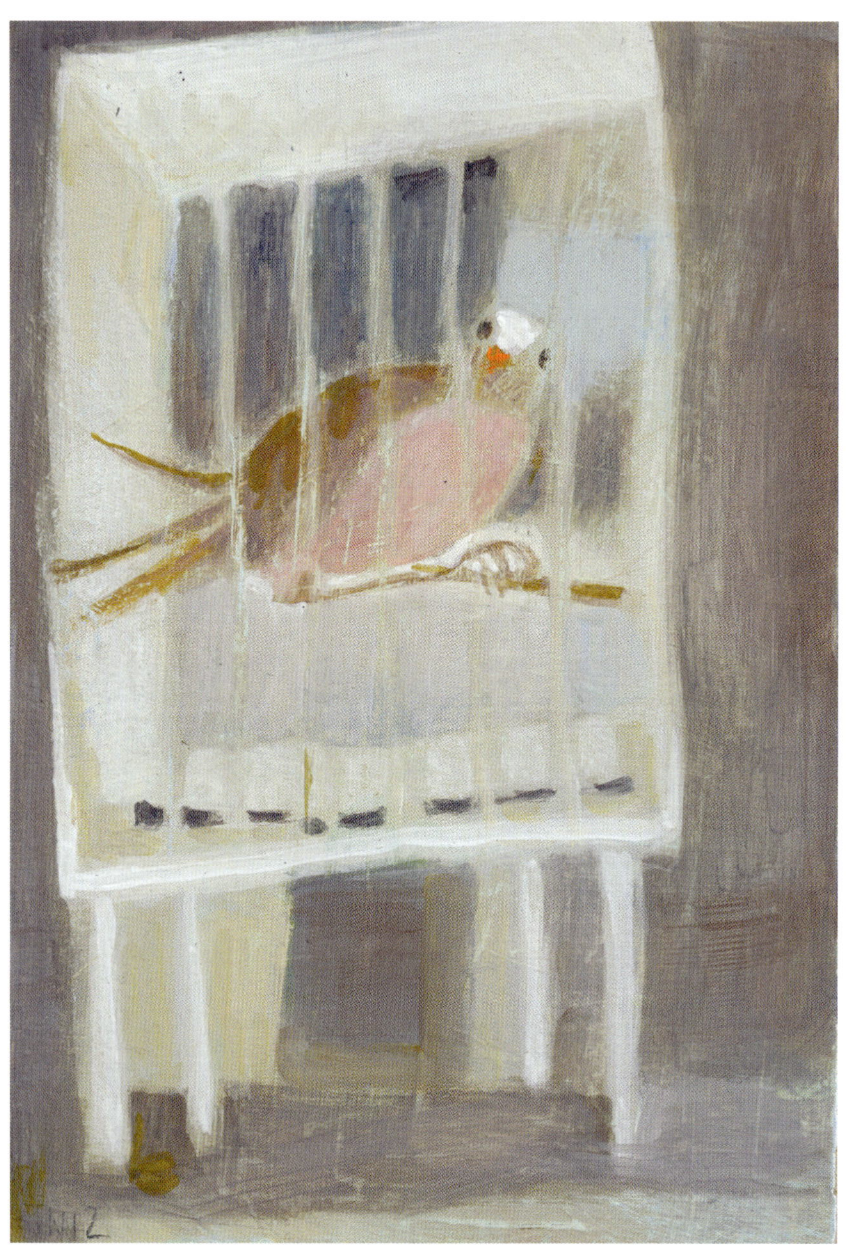

He's Looking at You, 2012, oil on board, 5½ x 3¾ inches

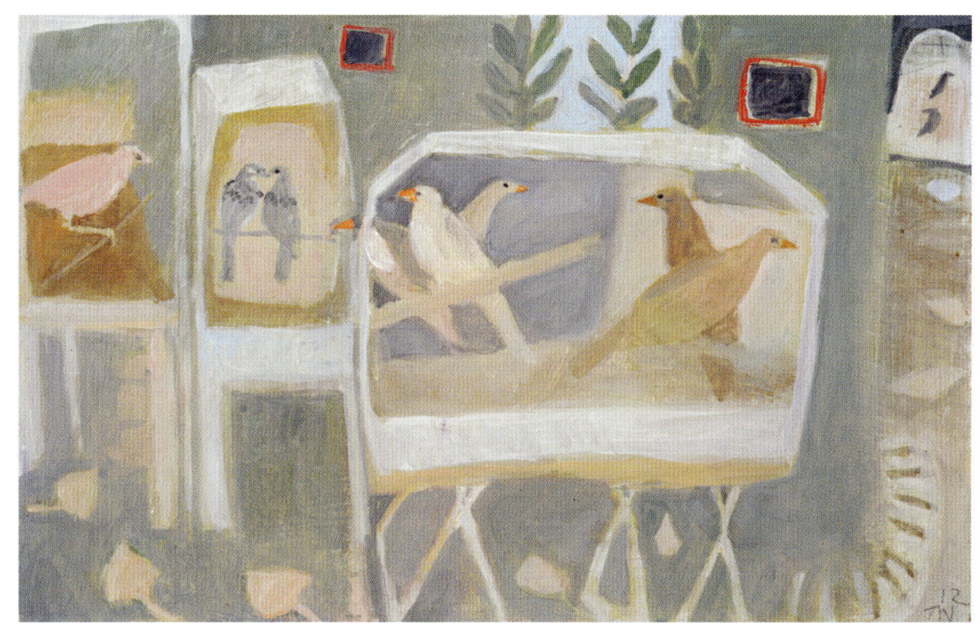

Bird Market, 2012, oil on board, 4¾ x 7¾ inches

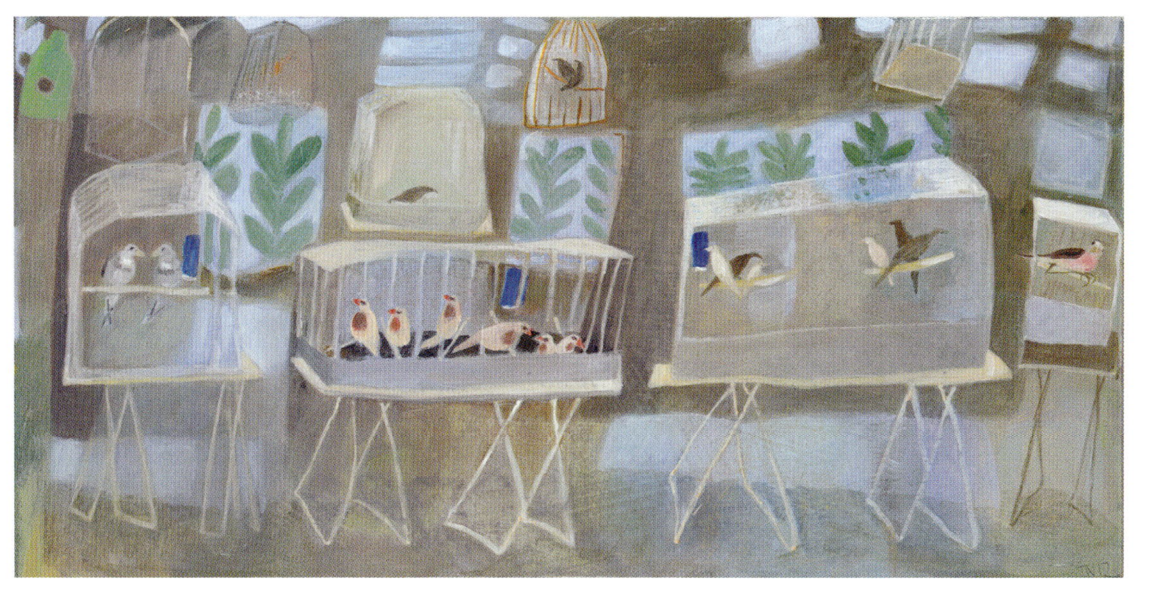

The Longer Bird Market, 2012, oil on board, 9½ x 19 inches

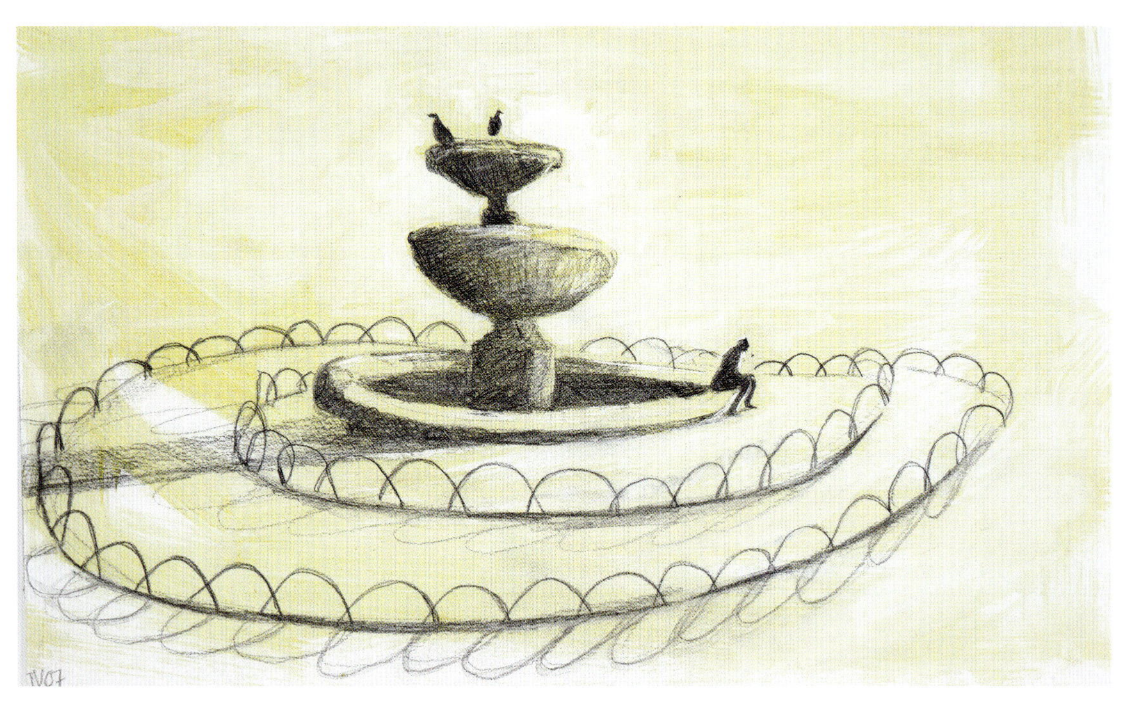

The Fountain, 2007, pencil and watercolour, 7 x 11½ inches

CHAPTER 4

Spaces

It is pleasant to sit on the Grand Boulevards –
The smell of
Cloacoe
Hot indiarubber
Poudre de riz
Algerian tobacco

(From Hope Mirrlees, 'Paris, A Poem', 1919)

Because the Paris *parcs* are so well-ordered, they allow you a breathing space to gather your thoughts. Their manicured trees require that you take up a good posture as you sit beneath them. In the summer though you can lie on those benches beneath the silver lindens. Sit, be lulled by fountains and children playing, thoughts ordered by the raked gravel, guarded by formidable railings capped with gold, the city revolving outside.

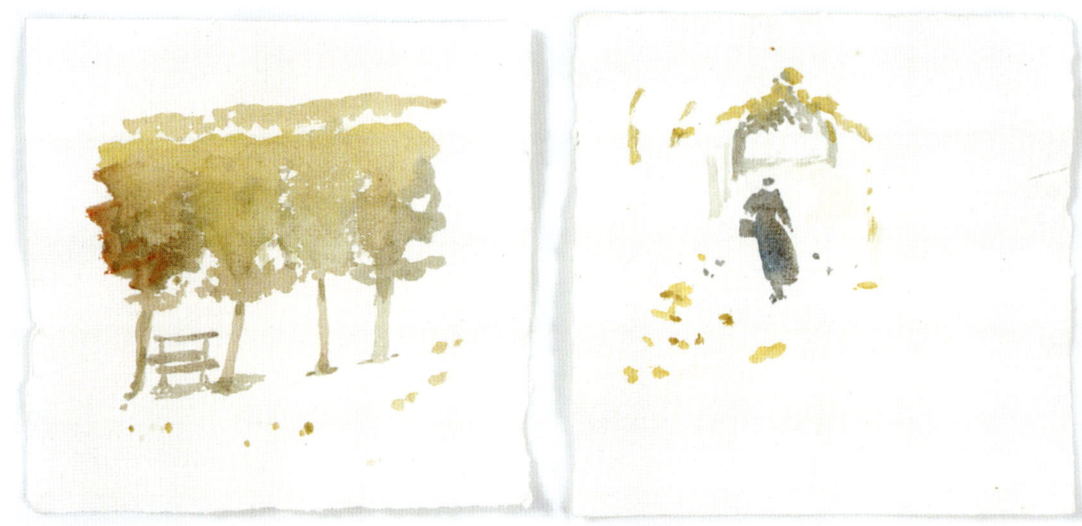

Avenue, 2012, watercolour, 2 sheets, each 6 x 6 inches

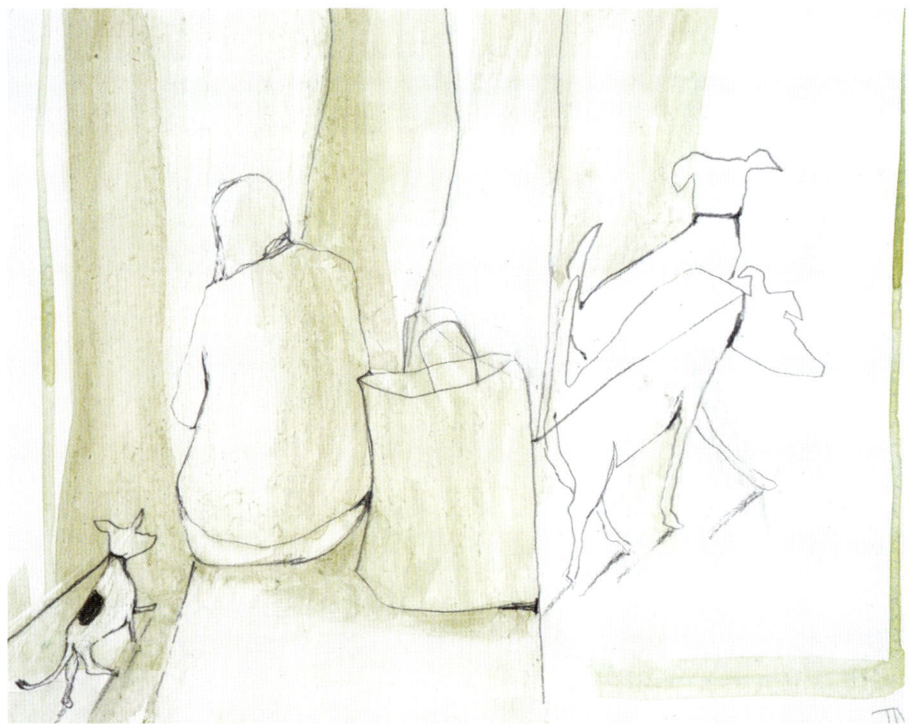

Pippin, 2011, pencil and watercolour, 6 x 7½ inches

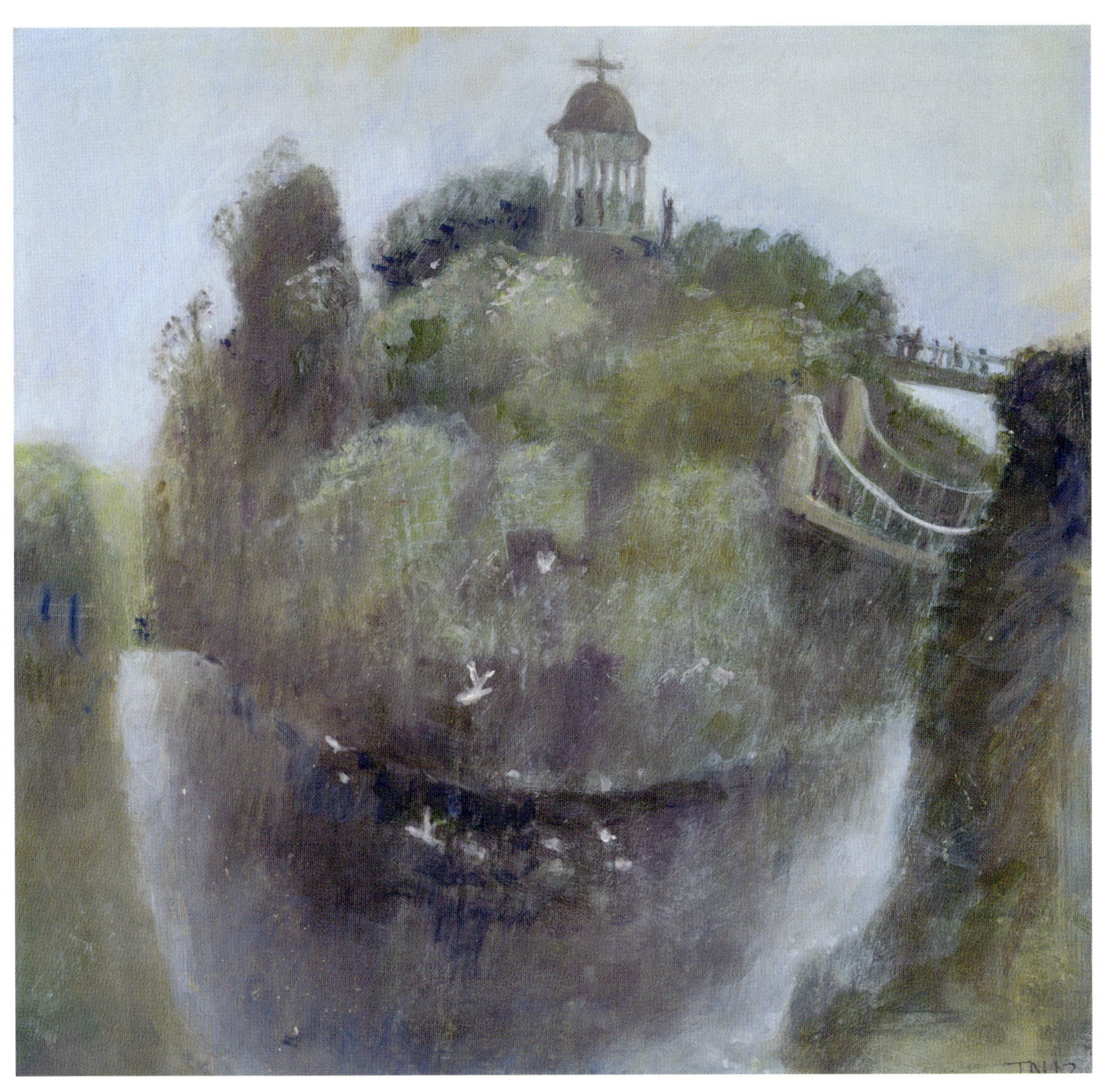

Hallo Henry (Buttes Chaumont), 2012, oil on board, 9 x 9 inches

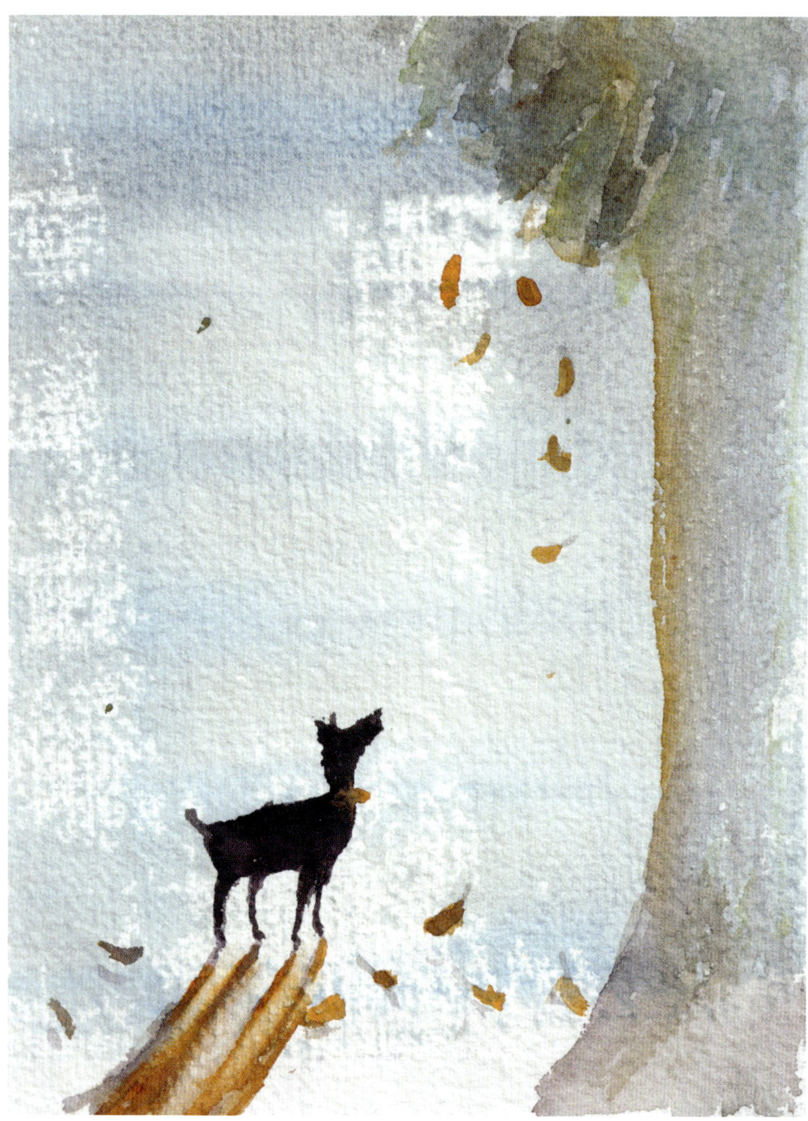

Looking at Falling Leaves, 2012, watercolour, 7½ x 5½ inches

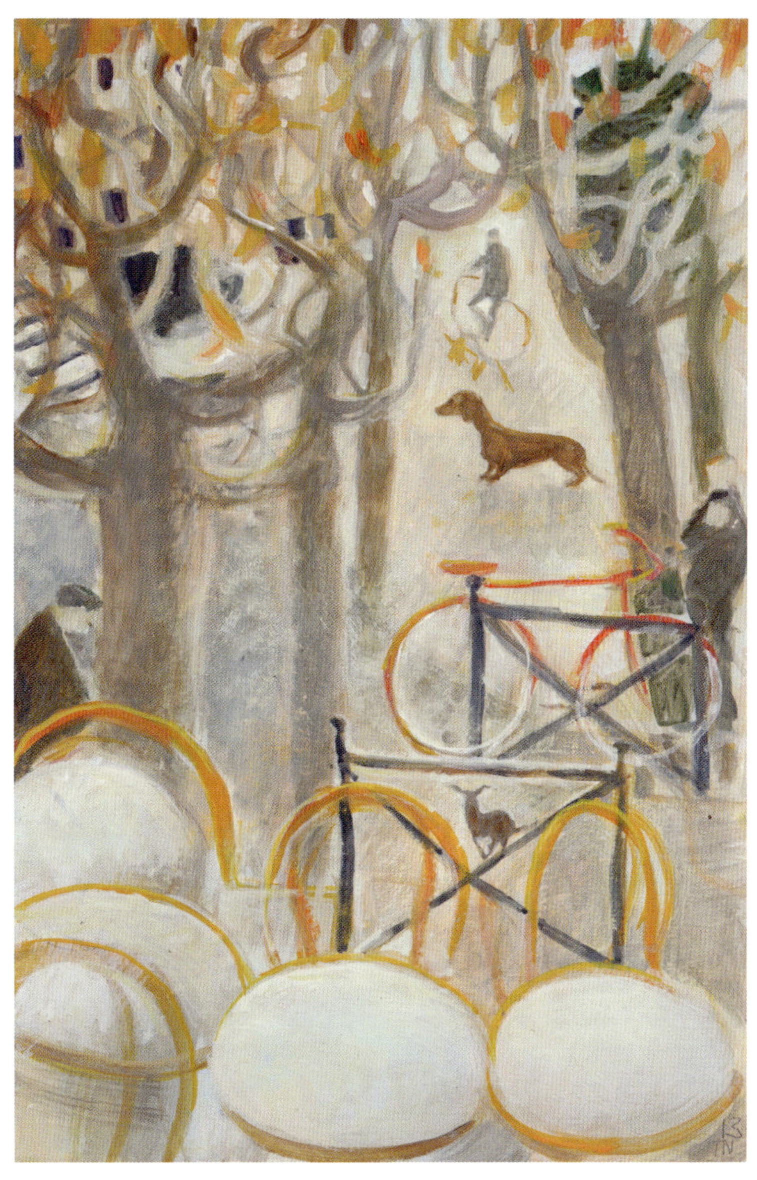

Copper Like the Saucepans, 2013, oil on board, 13½ x 8½ inches

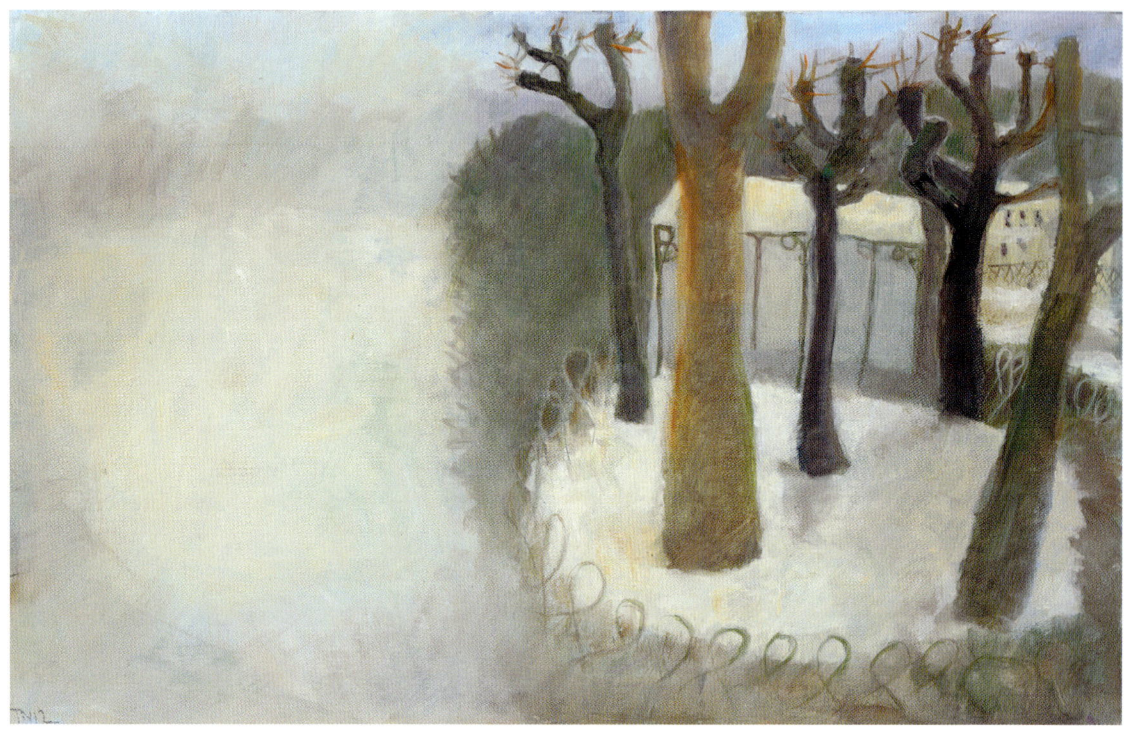

Snow in Playground, 2012, oil on board, 9 x 14 inches

Émile Zola has a lovely description of Paris in the snow. One New Year's Day the people wake up to find the city covered in a blanket of white: *All the ugliness of winter has disappeared; each house is like a beautiful woman in white furs*; and he writes of the *Seine flowing black, sinister, between two bands of dazzling white.* A barge passes loaded with snow like a chunk of the bank broken off and carried along with the current.

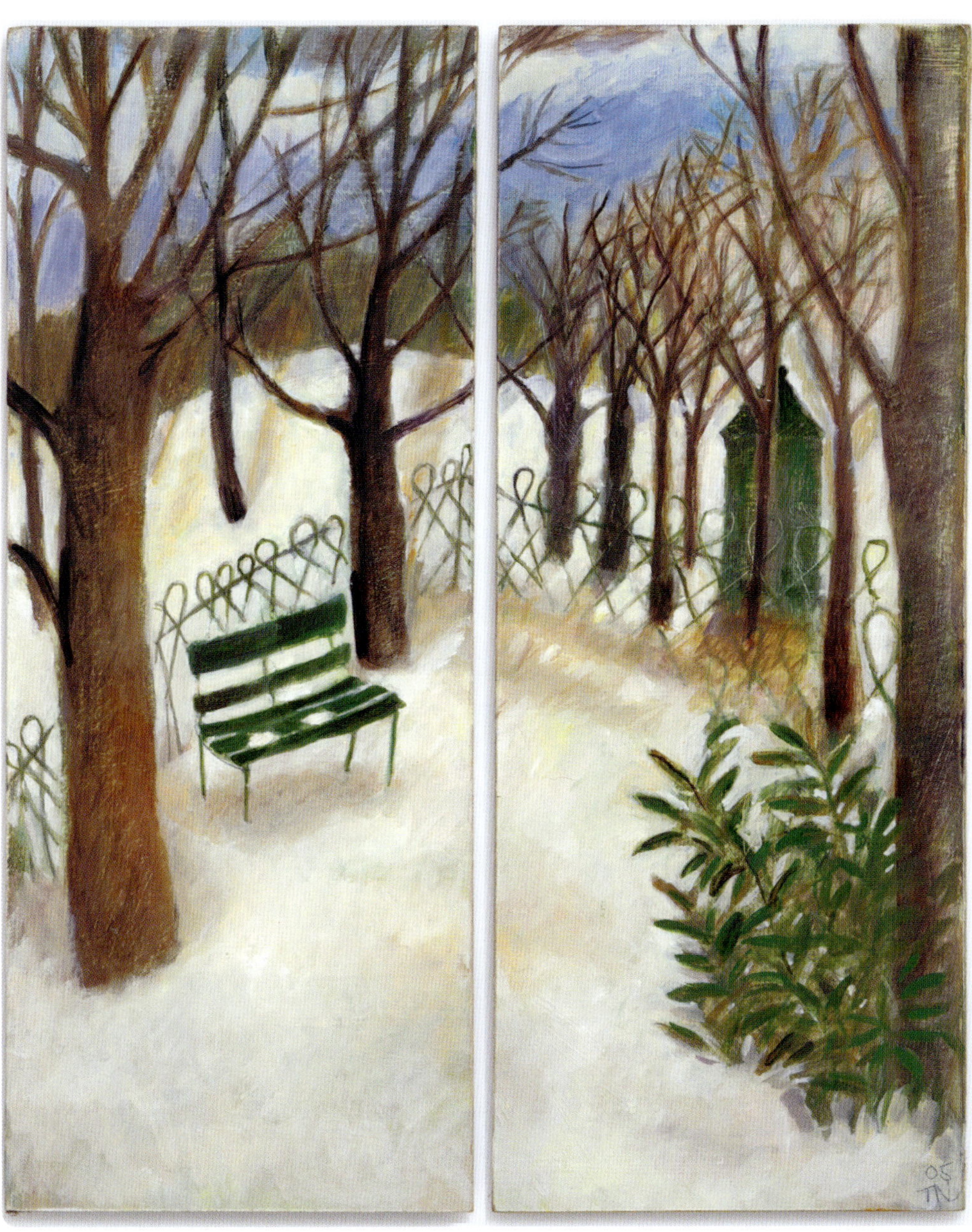

Snow, 2005, oil on board, 2 parts, total 12 x 11 inches

Place de Furstenberg

An exquisite square with a few trees on a small central island. Huge
handkerchief leaves shade us from a bright sky, letting through hovering discs of sunlight. A large husky dog on a dusty day darkens some
parched soil with its pee. I think about dogs in apartments. A group of
tourists assemble, they are told to look up when they want to sit down.
They shuffle offstage. Then, for a moment, the pigeons fold their wings,
and it's quiet.

Delacroix's garden

After the turbulence of Delacroix's dramatic paintings in the museum
– reds, golds, lions and war – women descend the iron staircase to sit
in this quiet courtyard garden with its bushes and fig trees and their
thoughts of home.

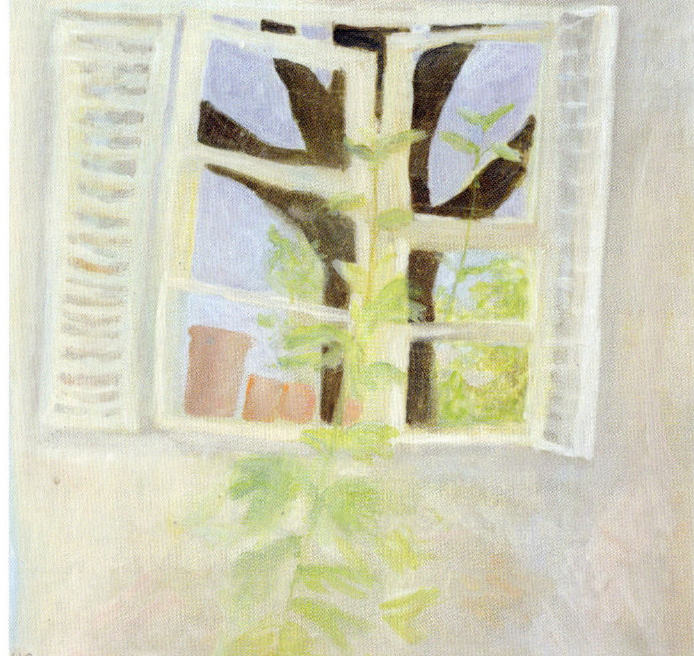

Window Reflecting Sky, 2012
oil on board
9 x 9¼ inches

Place Dauphine

As you walk across the Pont Neuf, turn into this quiet triangular square, that is easily missed, on the Île de la Cité. I found she was everything I wanted her to be. A spacious, empty square – except for an attractive man. Tall houses, well-groomed trees and combed sand. Cool benches and smart restaurants, thankfully shut.

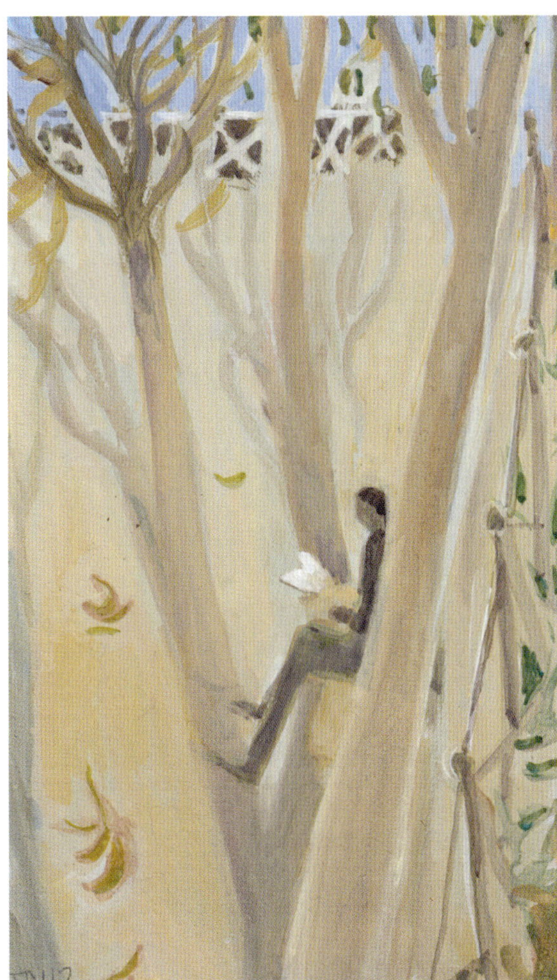

Knees Between Trees, 2012
oil on board
6¾ x 4 inches

An older woman had sat for long – leaves fell.

The Place de Tertre looked like a carnival. It was crowded with foreign tourists sitting at the café tables which occupied the entire square. Some poor devils, trying to look like artists, were peddling their portfolios of watercolours from table to table. There were musicians and street singers and on the corner was even a fire-eater in a skin-tight sailor's sweater.
(From *Les volets verts* by Georges Simenon, 1950)

Luxembourg Gardens

People in the Luxembourg Gardens. I imagine the small apartments they come from. This is their garden, their café and their sitting room.

There are many things to do in the Luxembourg Gardens. Fountains and carousels – sandpits, boules and chess.

A woman came along and arranged a table, with her chess pieces, and two chairs. Soon she was joined by an elderly man. They murmured to themselves, he occasionally breaking into song, with which she would join in – as they played their afternoon game in the space they had created.

Chess, 2012, oil on board, 8 x 15 inches

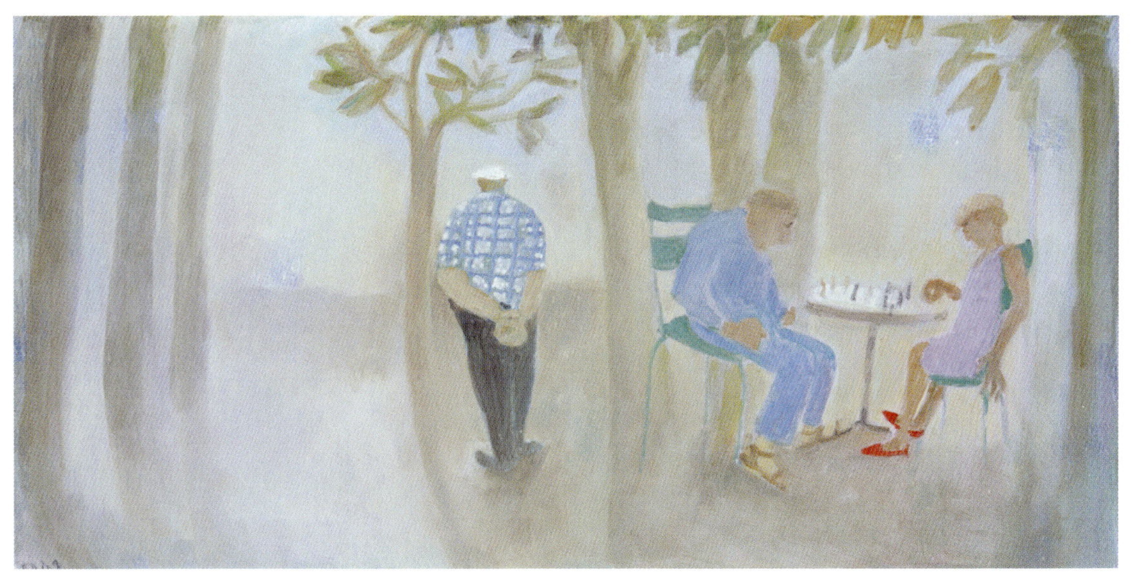

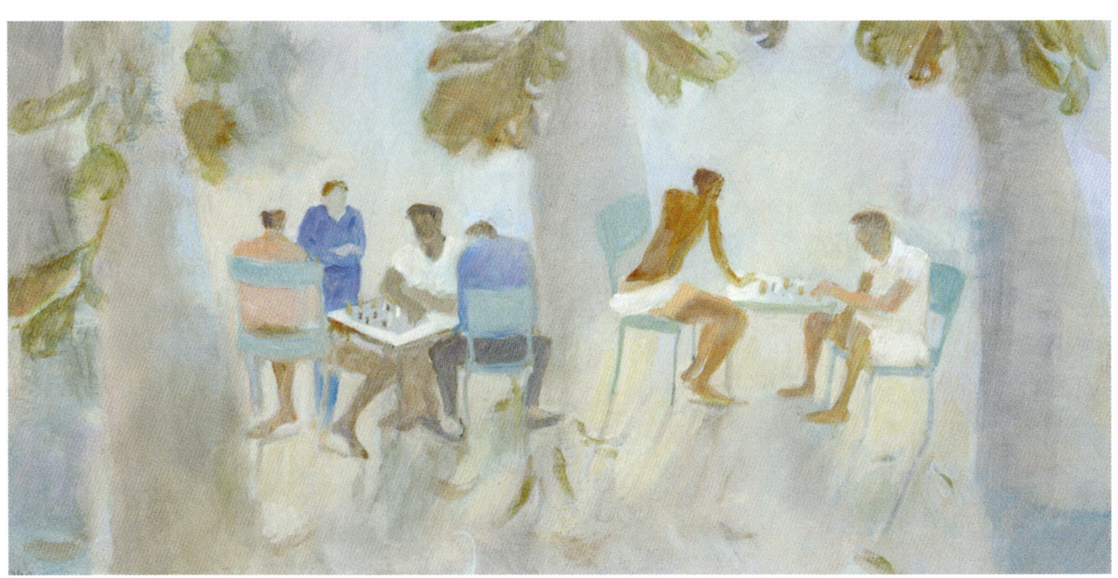

Chess Players, 2012, oil on board, 7 x 13¼ inches

In the furthest corner of the gardens is a small orchard of extremely espaliered fruit trees. Some have died under the rigid regime. Strange fruit hang from these trees – when I get closer, I see they are muslin bags tied carefully round each fruit to protect them from wasps, and each tree has on its name-tag a poem – Poire d'Ange, Caillot Rosa, Chat Rôti, Beurre d'Angleterre, Orange Musquée, Bon Chrétien d'Hiver, and Belle de Juin.

The poplar buds are golden chrysalids,
The Ballet of green Butterflies will soon begin.
(From Hope Mirrlees, 'Paris: A Poem', 1919)

The little tight chestnut buds that Jack stole from the Luxembourg Gardens have, in warm water and salt, swelled, abusted of themselves & turned into the most exquisite small dancing green stars. Too lovely for words.
(From a letter by Katherine Mansfield, 8 April 1922)

Parc Monceau

It's early December. The light is going, the trees bare. All sorts of
people are out in this strange parc. Muffled shuffles of approaching
runners and children's cries. Paths meander to various follies – a Dutch
windmill, a Chinese fort, an Egyptian pyramid, Corinthian pillars
round a dark pond.

The elderly man walking past rather painfully – is he being led by his
housekeeper? – is he eager to get back home so he can settle down in
his armchair in that sitting room with dimmed lights and heavy
curtains, pleased to have done his afternoon walk? A girl with long legs
and long fingers carries a bunch of green flowers in lime-green cello-
phane. A small boy carries a stick, coated with gold from the setting
sun. Two dogs meet but their owners don't, and the runners run round
and round the outside.

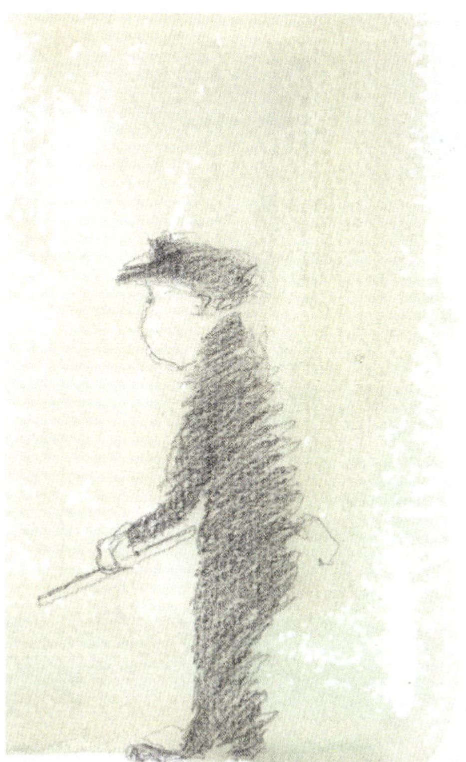

Boy with Stick, 2012
pencil and watercolour
5 x 3½ inches

Tuileries

Little boys in black overalls whose hands, sticky with
play, are like the newly furled leaves of the horse-
chestnuts ride round and round on wooden horses till
their heads turn.
(from Hope Mirrlees: 'Paris, A Poem', 1919)

In the Jardins des Tuileries carousels have
turned for many years and for many children. They can sit on the galloping horses,
go in the beeping cars or choose the ostrich
with his long neck, silly face and large floppy
feet forever running. Uncomfortable as if he
doesn't want to be there. I know a man who
dreams of this ostrich.

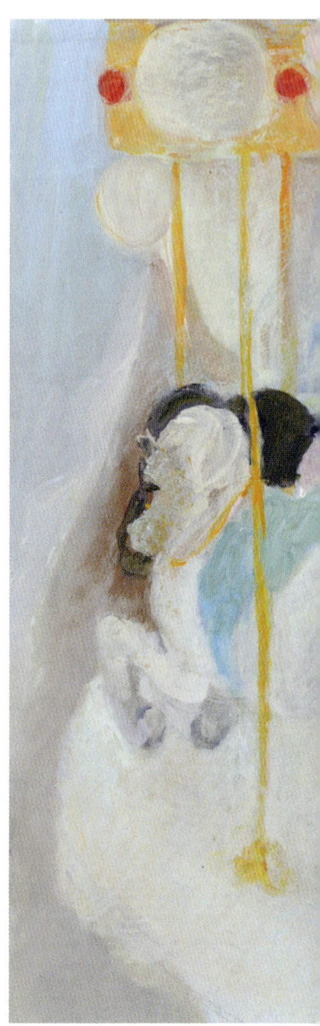

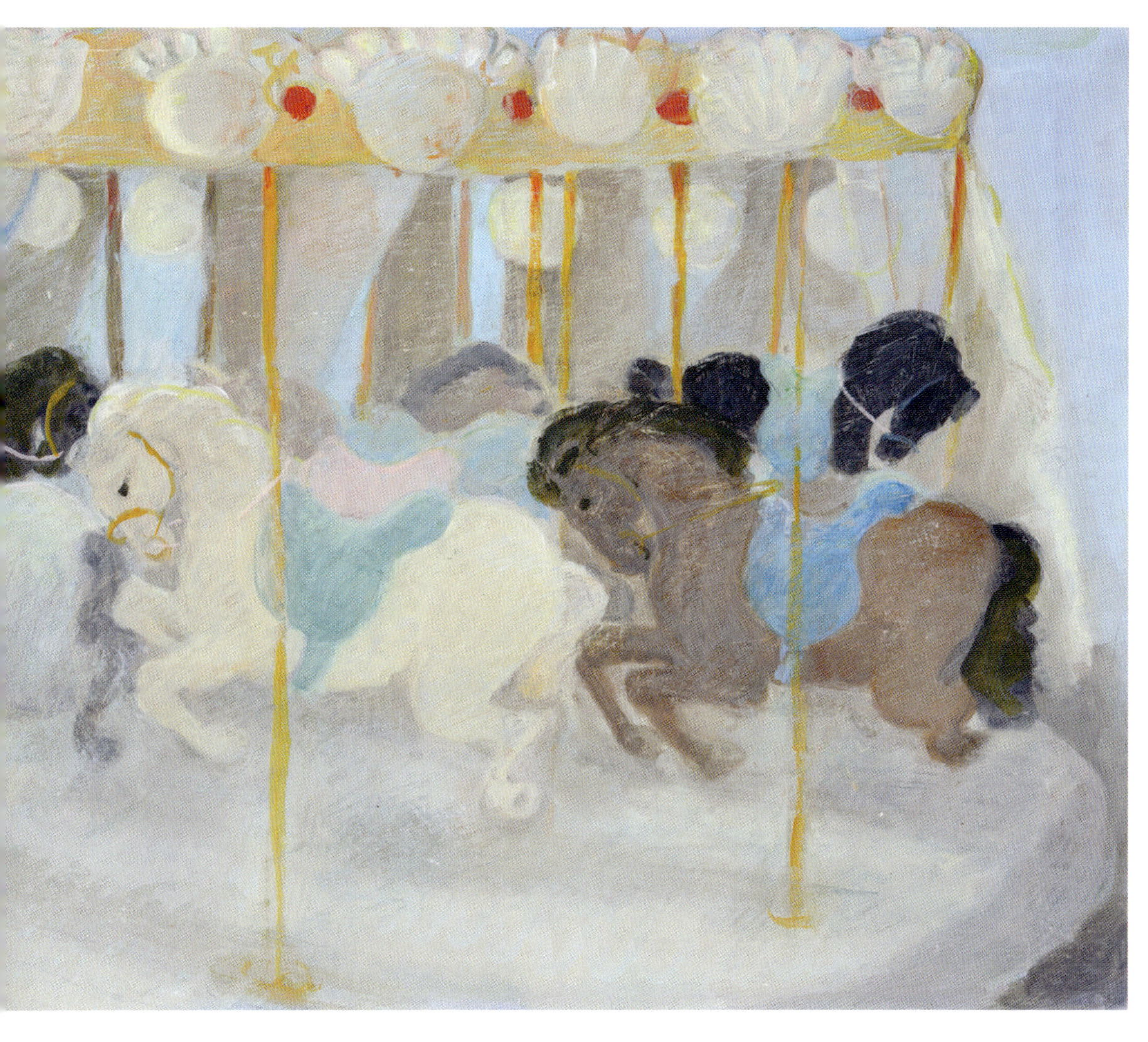

Carousel, 2011, oil on board, 10 x 15 inches

The carousel continued its mood of fixed jollity

Proust

I took my son to Paris, or rather, I paid
and he took me – he being 24 and
more *au fait* with google maps and
smart phones. I asked him if he liked
Paris. He said 'I love it all' and
photographed everything. By the time
we got to the Tuileries it was dusk and
drizzling. I was ready for my cup of tea
when he asked, 'What is Proust about,
then?' I managed something about
memories and madeleines.

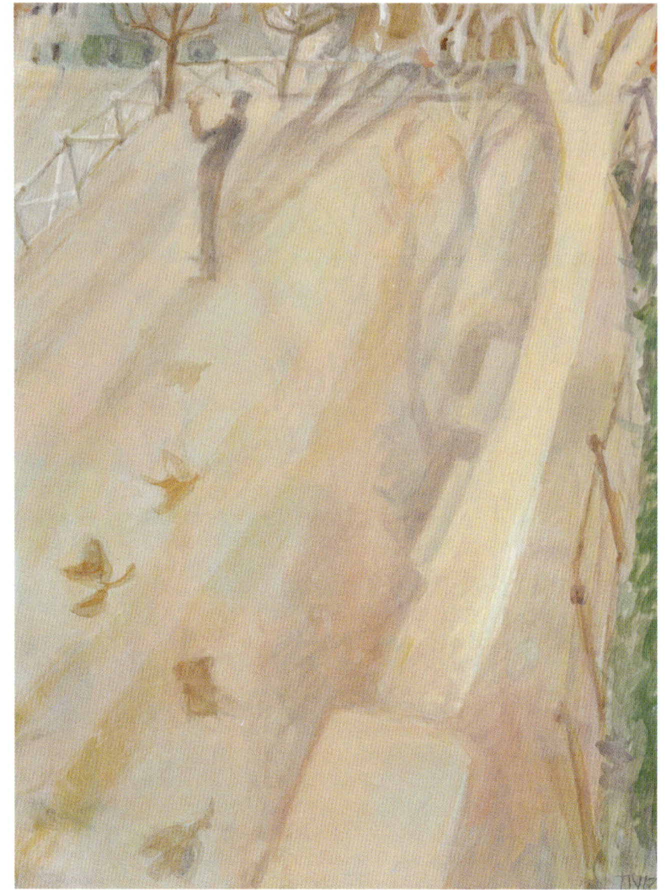

The Digital Pose, 2012, oil on board, 12½ x 9 inches

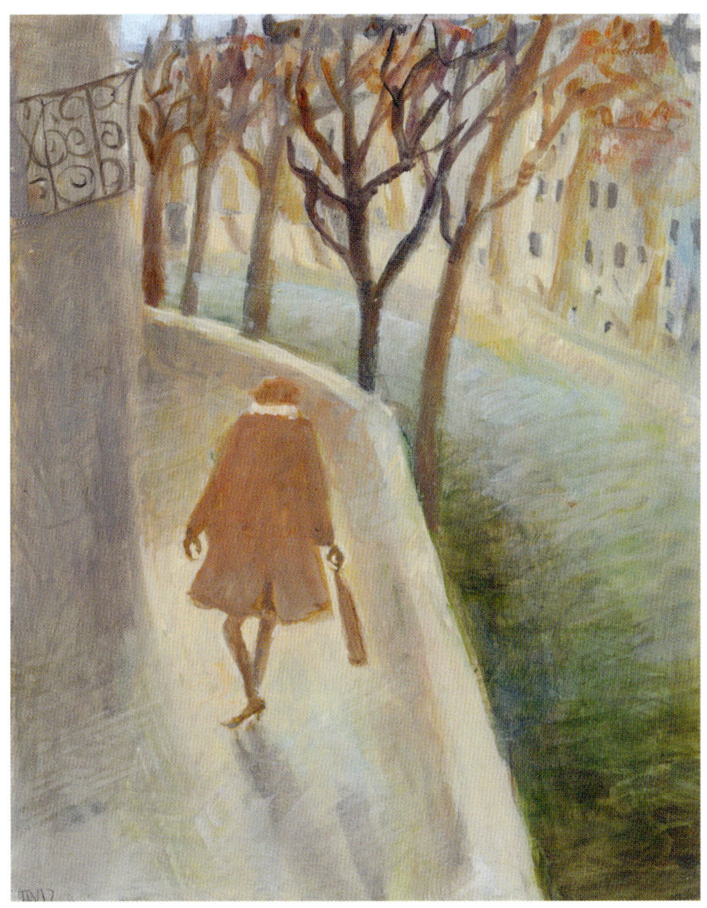

Seine, 2012, oil on board, 9½ x 7 inches

The Seine

What can I say about the Seine? I look down into its dark green water.
It's cold this side. The trees are bare. It's gold on the other side in the sun.
There the shadows of the trees are stronger than the trees themselves.

The Seine, old egotist,
meanders imperturbably
towards the sea,
Ruminating on weeds and rain...
(from Hope Mirrlees: 'Paris, A Poem', 1919)

On a Sunday afternoon

Mostly *bateaux-bus* ploughed the Seine. Annoying tannoys. But then there were two barges – straight from an Impressionist painting. The first was loaded with ballast. Its features were picked out in peppermint green. The next carried containers – lovely coloured boxes – tomato reds, buffs, soft greens, burnt umbers. These colours dulled as it slipped into the shadows of the bridge. A girl in a white dress slipped into the shadows of a tunnel along the quay. On this heat-wave after-noon, a young man lay asleep on the concrete edge of the river, its flowing riband of swimming pool colours transporting him elsewhere.

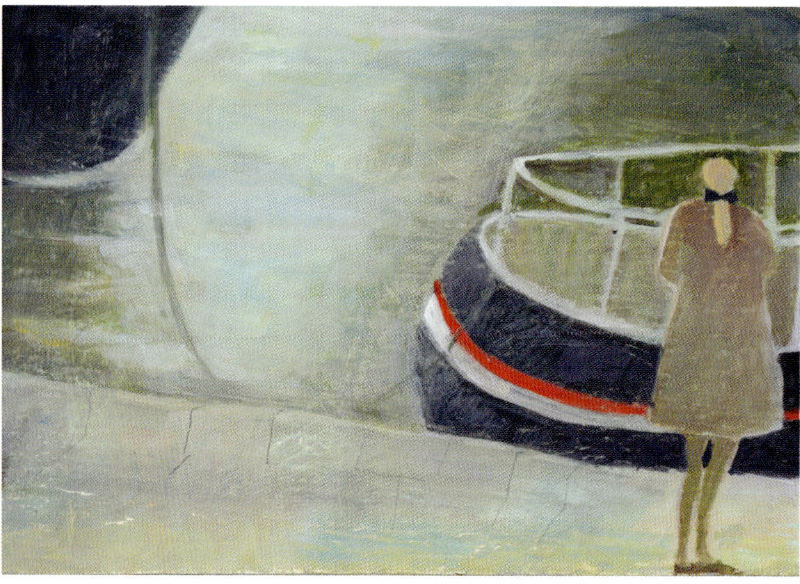

Tied Up, 2012, 6¼ x 8½ inches

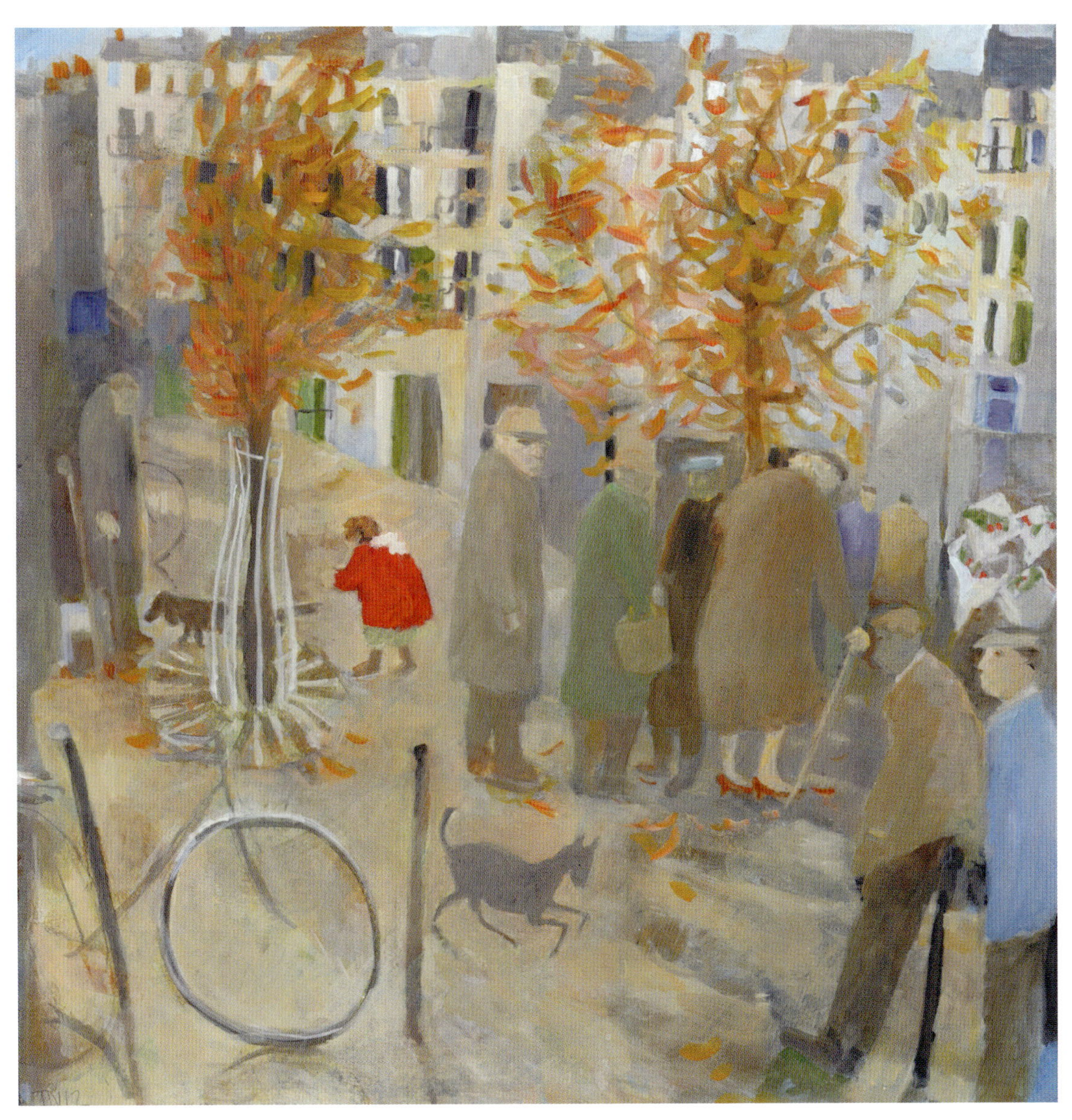

Sunday, 2012, oil on board, 13½ x 13 inches

The Palais Royal for all its grandeur has some pretty cramped spaces.

*A friend was managing one of those exclusive galleries in the arcades.
It had been designed by an architect to double as a living space. Walls
moved and revealed shelving; another moved and there were the cooking
facilities. Stairs to the mezzanine projected from the wall looking like an
art exhibit. At the top, the guest bed folded out and rested on top of a
desk. The master bedroom had an en-suite shower in a cupboard; an
oriel window looked out over the courtyard.*
Ken Skipper

Palais Royal. Floating pools of light.
And, at the top, urns that could topple.

Colette lived in the Palais Royal (as did Cocteau). At first not in a
grand apartment but on a mezzanine. These low rooms are tucked
above the shops, below the apartments. Sometimes they are used as
storerooms. As they are in the arcade they don't have a view across the
square – only of the top of people's heads and their muffled footfall.
Nor is there any direct light, only that reflecting up from the pavement. Later she moved up to 9, rue de Beaujolais, a proper apartment,
nearly above Le Grand Véfour, a grand restaurant. In her later days,
meals were carried up to her or she was carried down to them.

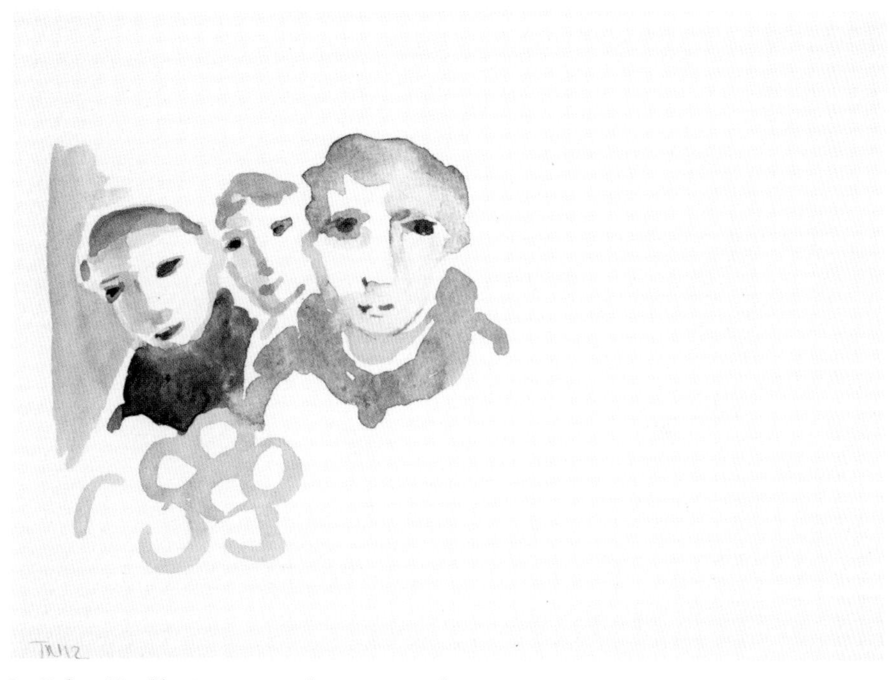

Les Enfants Terribles, 2012, watercolour, 5¼ x 7 inches

Madame Colette once said to me one needn't read *the great poets, for they give off an atmosphere. It is truly very strange, too, that we poets can read one another, as Rilke says. With a friend to help with the words, I can read Shakespeare in English, but not the newspaper.*

(Jean Cocteau interviewed by William Fifield in *The Paris Review*, Summer-Fall, 1964)

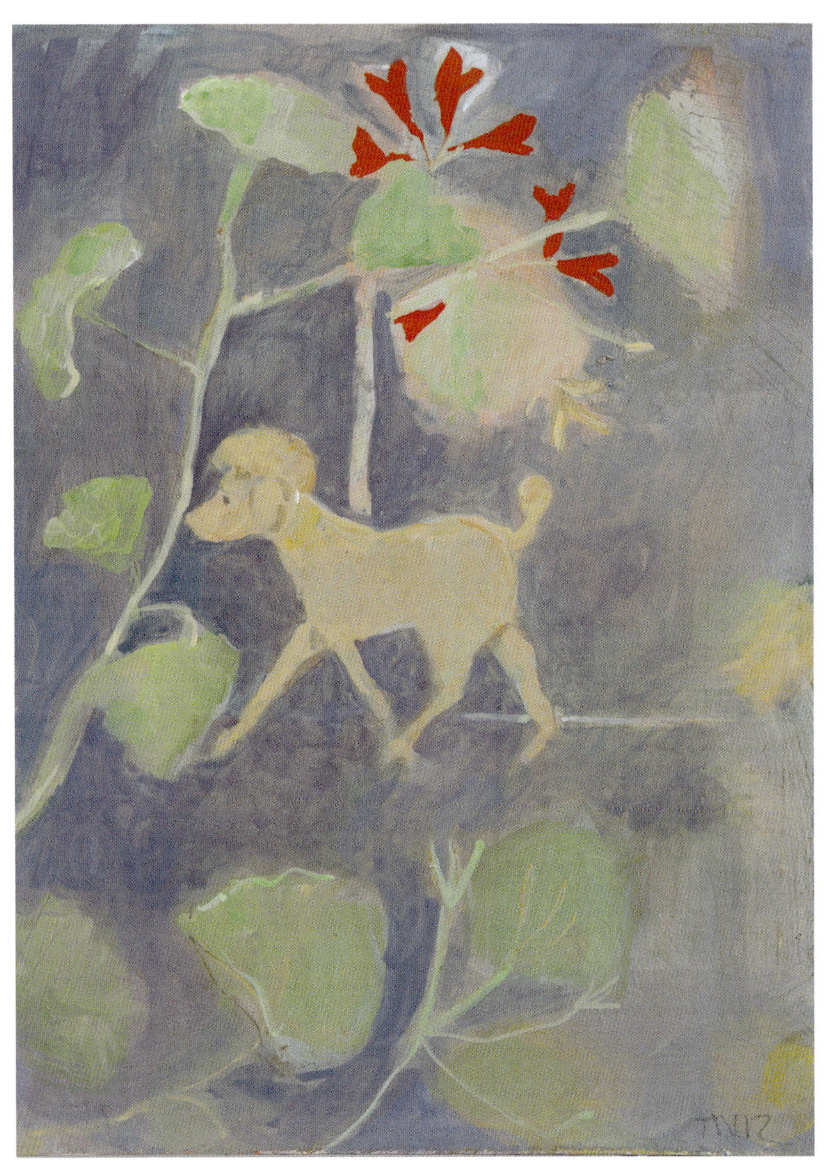

The Beige Poodle Walked Quickly Past the Chinese Takeaway, 2012, 7½ x 5½ inches

CHAPTER 5

Dogs

They say the smaller the dog the smarter the woman but small dogs can get trodden on or tripped over, causing an accident, either to the dog or to its owner.

It's also good to have a large dog – to have both is very fashionable. Little dogs have always been popular. Yorkshire terriers seem to be in at the moment. One imagines all these little dogs in their apartments with their legs crossed waiting to come out and do their business at the base of a tree.

This season dogs are wearing: blue angora on a Highland terrier, a Norfolk terrier looking good in an old leather coat, and a Yorkshire terrier in Highland plaid.

Staccato

It's all very well these sweet little dogs trotted out in their coats, but they can be vicious. When my friend approached one, it yapped furiously. Poor little dog. It was probably just trying to defend itself.

Four days: three dachshunds, Yorkshire terriers, one Great Dane on the metro – no cats.

Dogs in the wrong places.

Horrid dog she put in a pram.

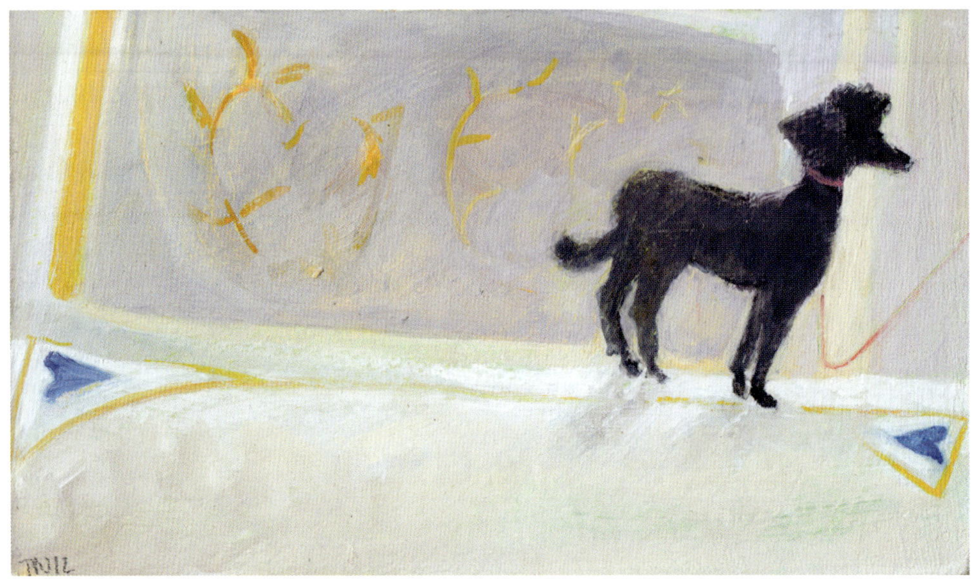

Having Her Nails Done, 2012, oil on board, 4¾ x 7½ inches

Crossing, 2012, oil on board, 6¾ x 8½ inches

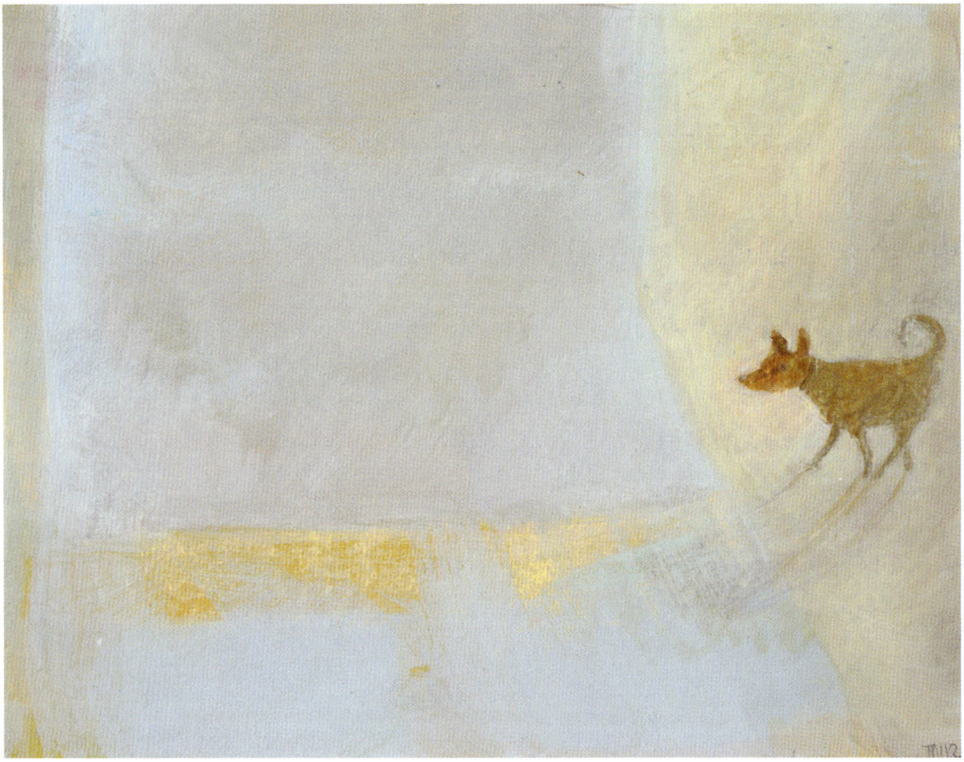

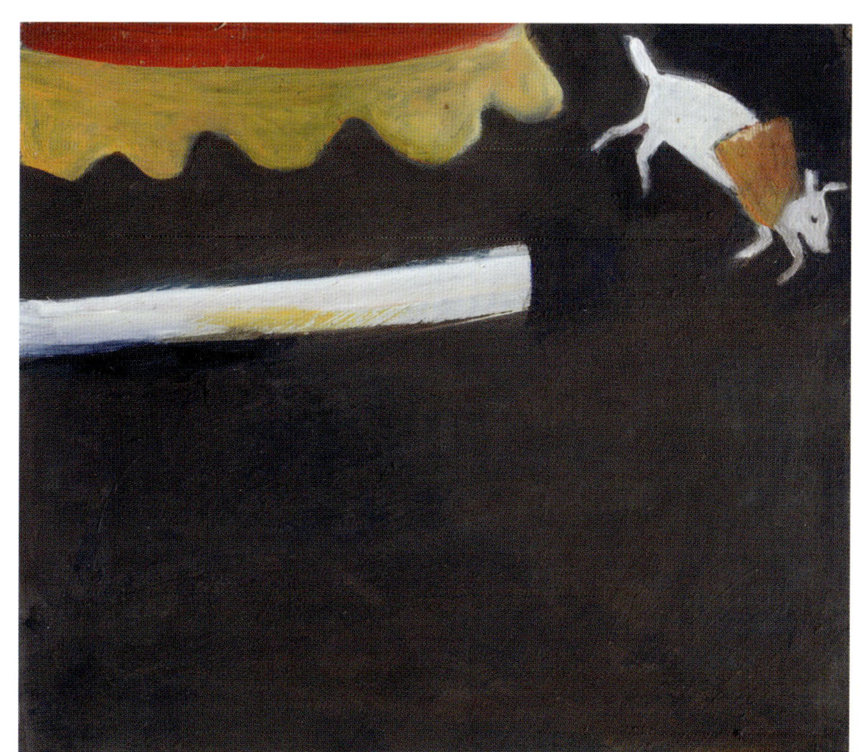

Super Dog, 2010
oil on board
4½ x 5¼ inches

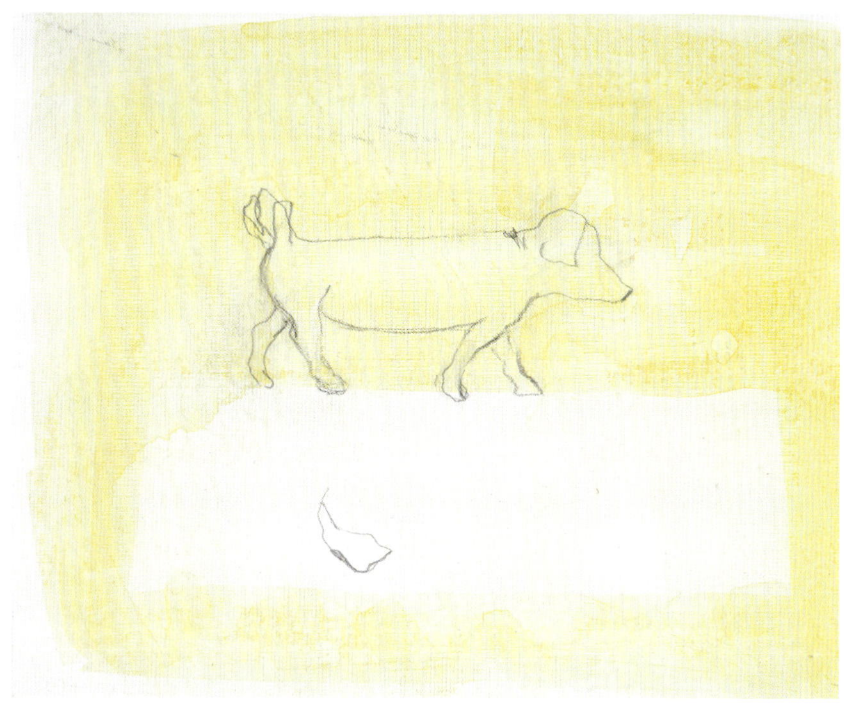

Sunset, 2011
pencil and watercolour
4¾ x 5 inches

Designer Bag and Dog, 2007, pencil and watercolour, 8¼ x 5½ inches

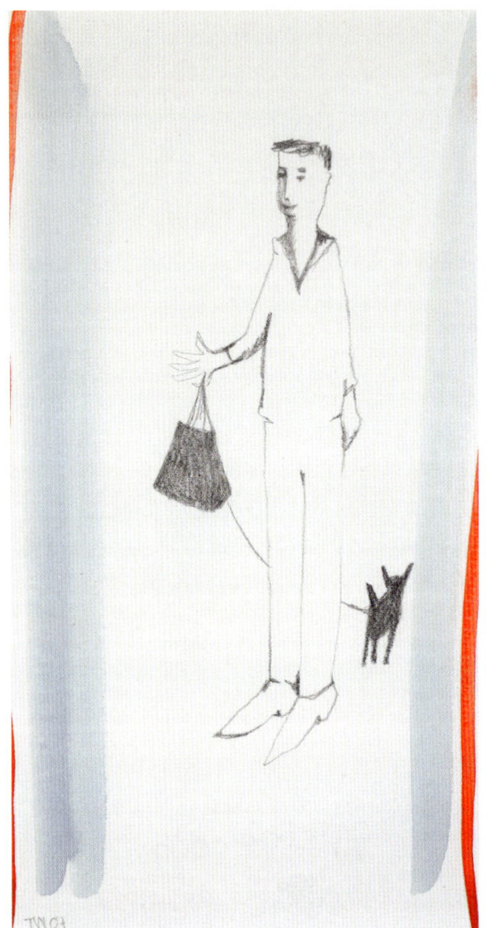

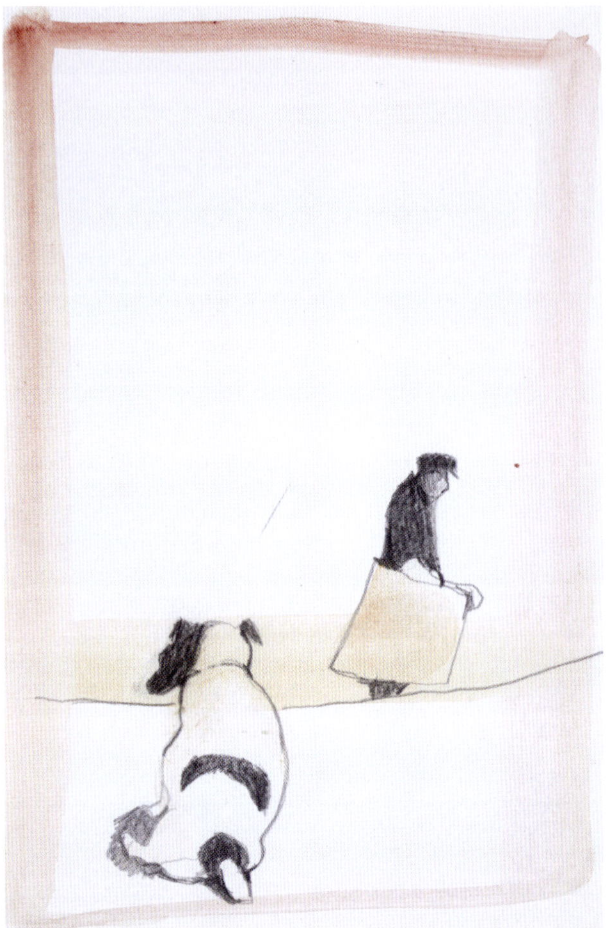

Portfolio, 2012, pencil and watercolour, 8¼ x 5¼ inches

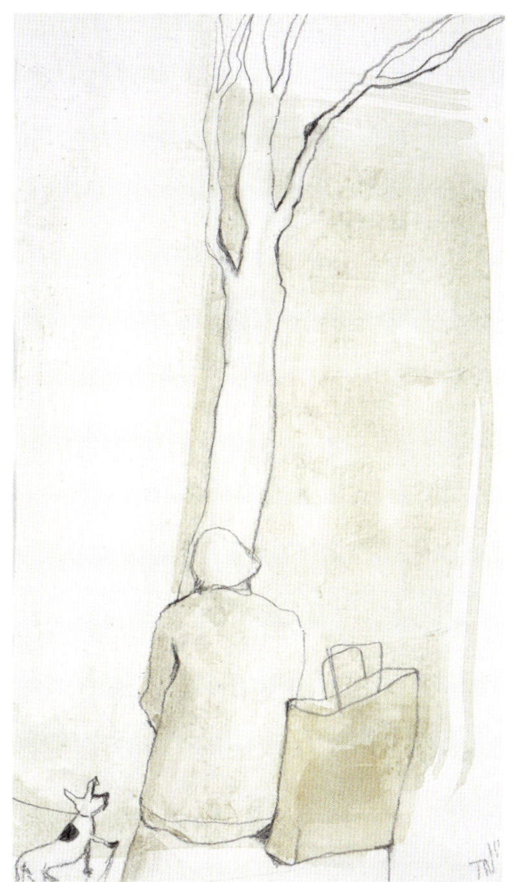

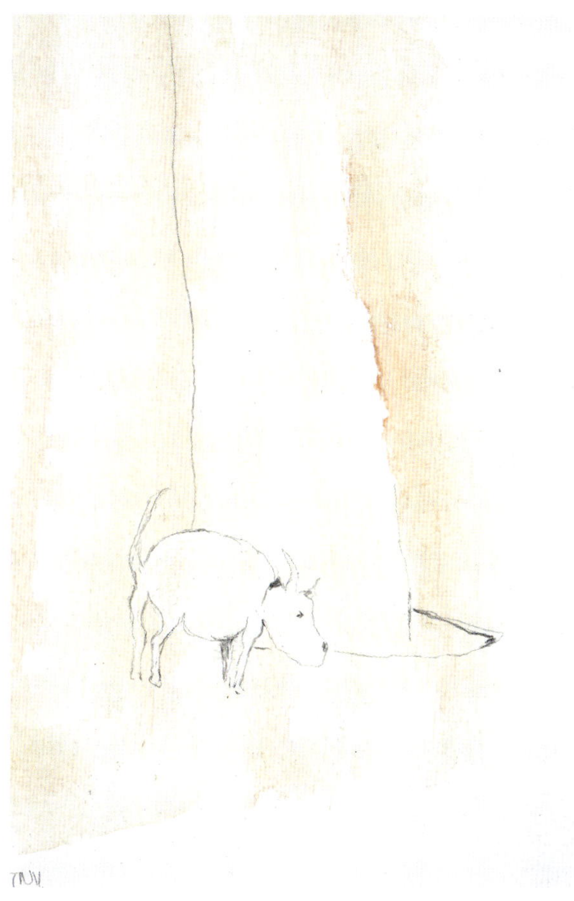

Saturday, Late Afternoon, 2011, pencil and watercolour, 7½ x 4 inches

At the Base of the Tree, 2011, pencil and watercolour, 8 x 5½ inches

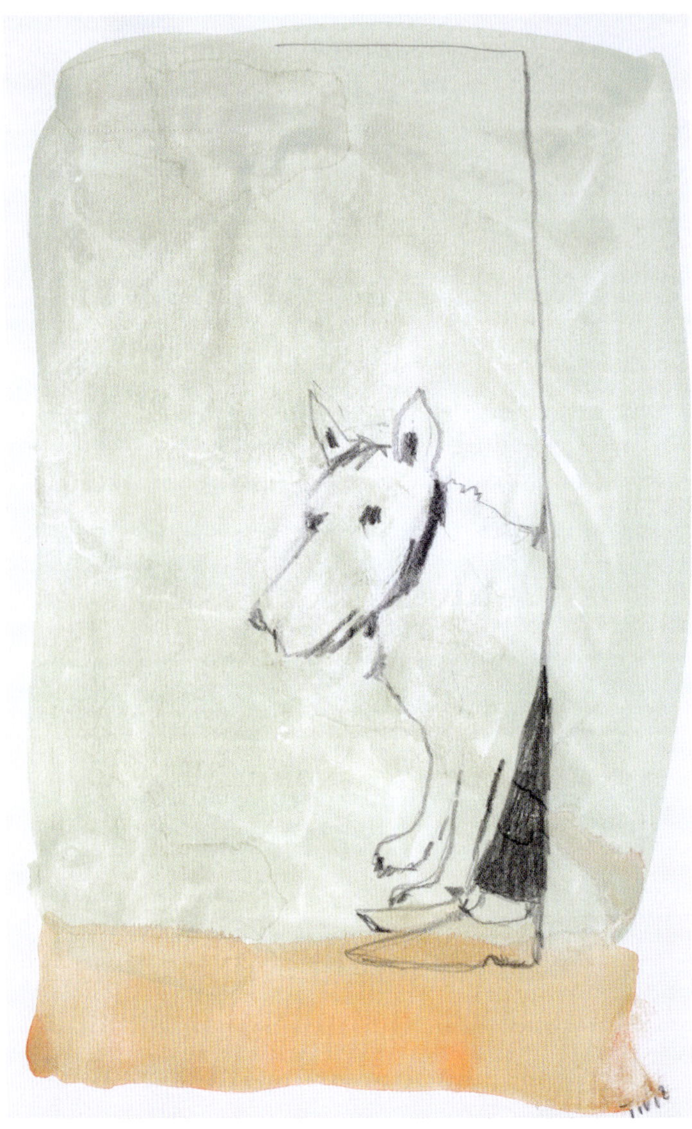

Like a Ginger Bear, 2010, pencil and watercolour, 8¼ x 5¼ inches

CHAPTER 6

Doorknobs

Paris is a world meant to be seen by the walker alone, for only the pace of strolling can take in all the rich (if muted) detail. The loiterer, the flâneur, has a long distinguished pedigree in France...

Baudelaire...compare[s] the flâneur to a mirror as huge as the crowd – or to a kaleidoscope outfitted with a consciousness that at every shake of the tube copies the configuration of multifarious life and the graceful movements of all its elements...
(from *The Flâneur: A Stroll through the Paradoxes of Paris* by Edmund White, 2001)

Moulded doors decorated at the bottom with kicks.
Decorative windows above, that no-one looks through or at.

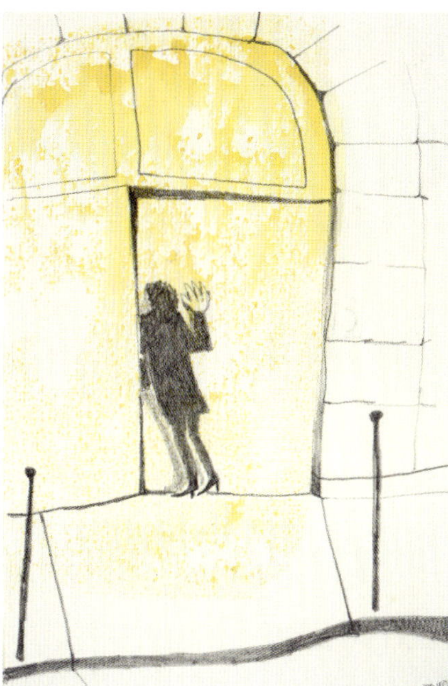

Girl Opening Door, 2010
pencil and watercolour
7½ x 5 inches

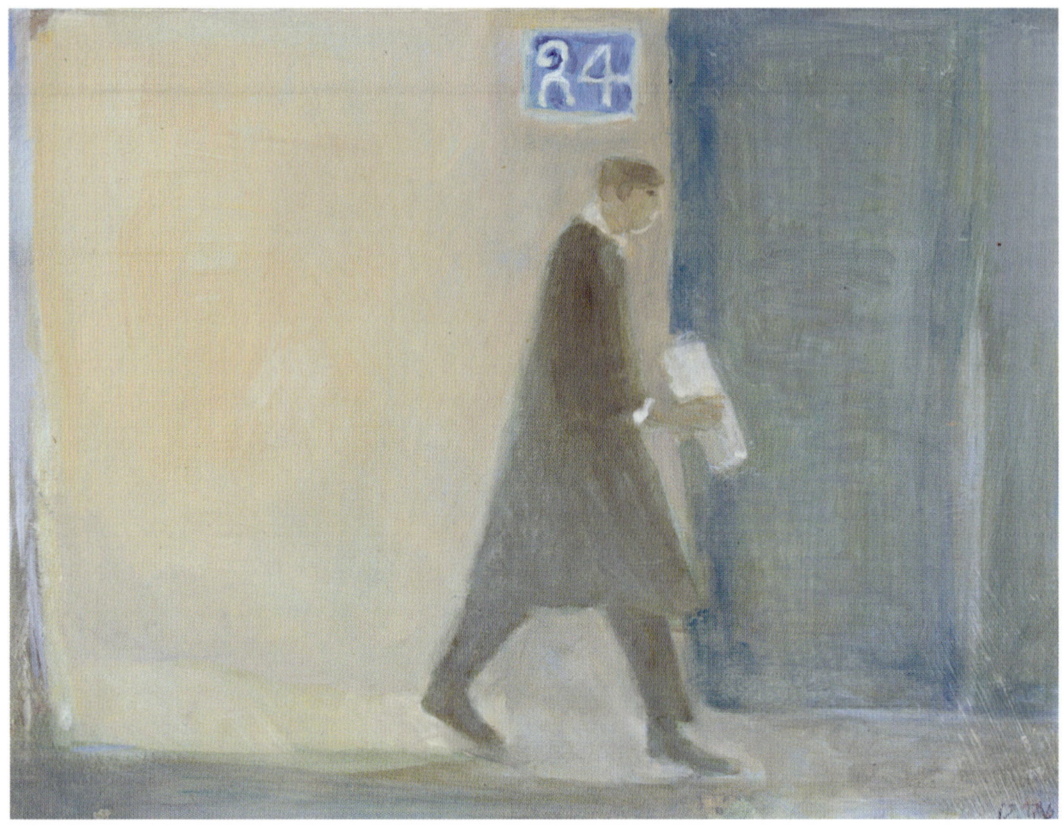

Cité of Blue Plaques, 2012, oil on board, 7 x 9 inches

Various people in the street

Down by the Canal Saint Martin on a warm Friday evening, only the people coming towards us were carrying baguettes.

People were coming out of an African restaurant to make mobile phone calls – each absorbed in their own play – making impressive theatrical gestures, echoed in their long shadows stretching down the street.

Elsewhere, the *flâneur* is on his mobile.

Apparently French women have better legs.

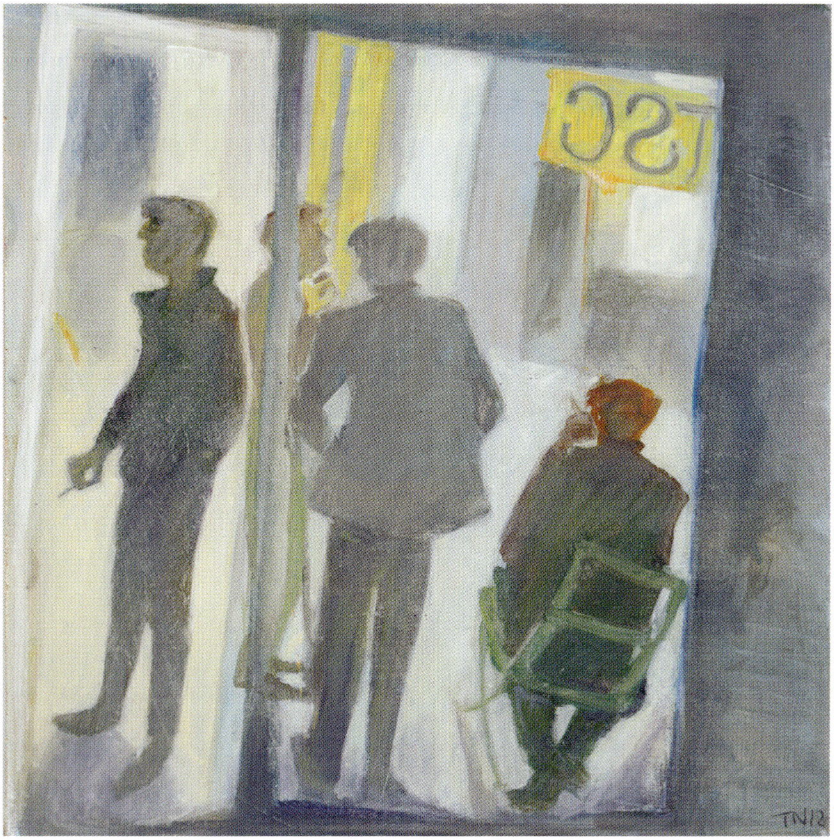

Men Smoke Outside, 2012
oil on board, 9 x 9 inches

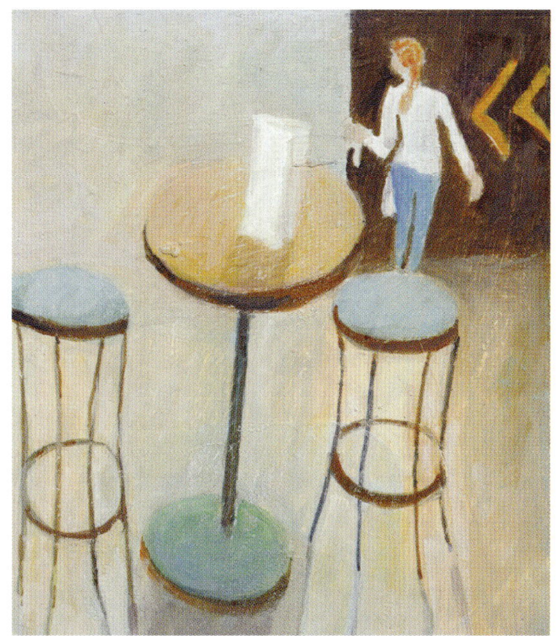

Legs, 2012
oil on board
5¾ x 4¾ inches

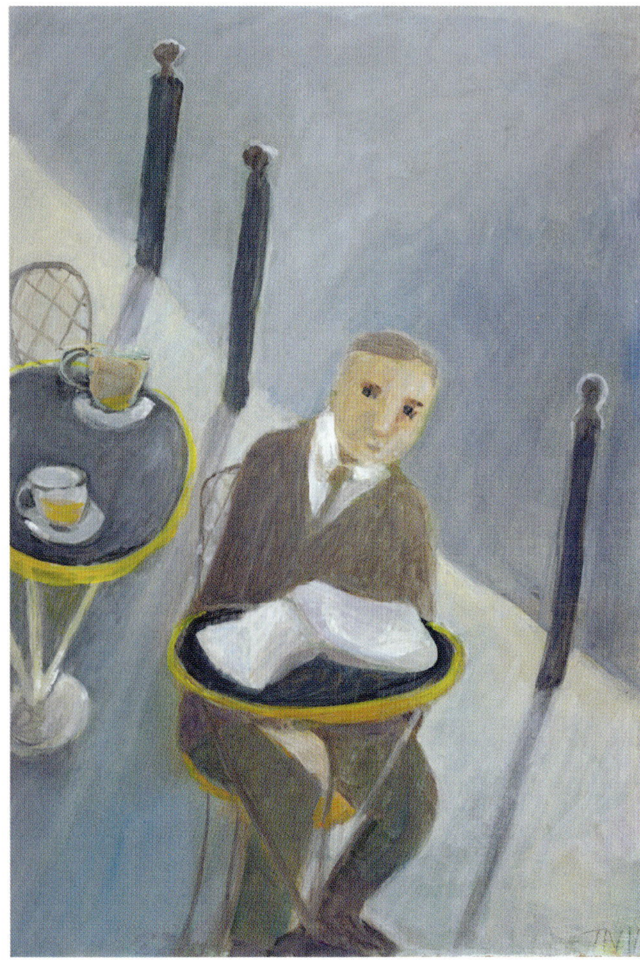
Then He Looked at Me, 2012
oil on board, 8¾ x 6 inches

It was a Sunday evening, early. An ordinary street in Le Marais, quiet. A taxi arrives. An overdressed groom overpays the taxi driver who then gives them his good wishes. The bride, holding her bouquet, turns to me – the only onlooker. We smile. He fumbles in his pocket for the key. Will he carry her across the threshold to her new life in that flat above the chemist's?

Thick gold bands round the café tables caught in the sun. They reminded me of large wedding rings.

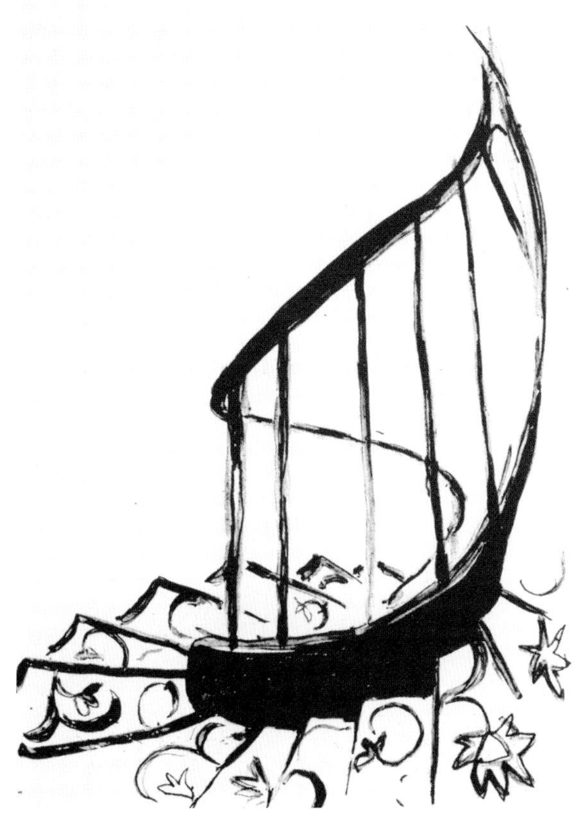

Spiral Staircase, 2007, lithograph, 9¼ x 7¼ inches, Curwen Press

Into the courtyard

There do seem to be a lot of spiral staircases in Paris. Step through one of those imposing courtyard doors and peep into one of the shared side entrances; however modest the apartments, there is often a marvellous spiral staircase complete with elaborate iron bannister, and the last stone step worn with years of people swinging round the bottom.

Staircases

In one apartment up and up a narrow staircase, the visitors' book said, 'The views quite take my breath away. So do the stairs.'

Balcony brassieres
and first floor
windows
Spiral staircases
turning like ribbon
off a roll.

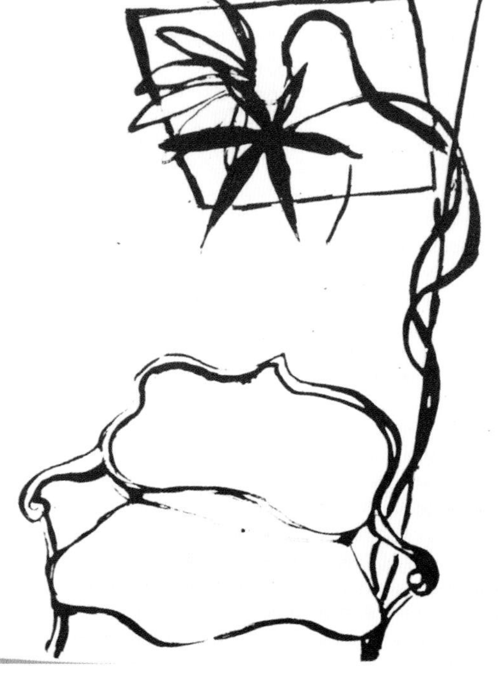

At the Top of the Stairs, 2007, two lithographs, each 9¼ x 7¼ inches, Curwen Press

Every enterprise
has its own set
of desires.
To enter a shop is
a walk-on part to
a particular drama.

Balcony Bras, 2007, two lithographs, each 9¼ x 7¼ inches, Curwen Press

Musée de Camondo

On the edge of Parc Monceau is the Musée Nissim de Camondo, an elegant house (built in 1911) filled with fine 18th-century French furniture and objêts d'art. An austere spiral staircase leads to elaborately decorated suites of rooms which were occupied by different members of the Camondo family. The kitchen – which then would have been a hub of steam, sweat and humanity – is half sunk underground, completely encased in tiles so no kitchen smells or servants' noises could escape. Only the food rises silently in a dumb waiter to the dining room above. The house became a museum in 1935. Now the kitchen utensils are laid out like surgical instruments. A meal of plaster food is set out in the servants' dining room but real plums sit in kilner jars on the draining board.

Plums, 2012, oil on card, 7 x 11¼ inches

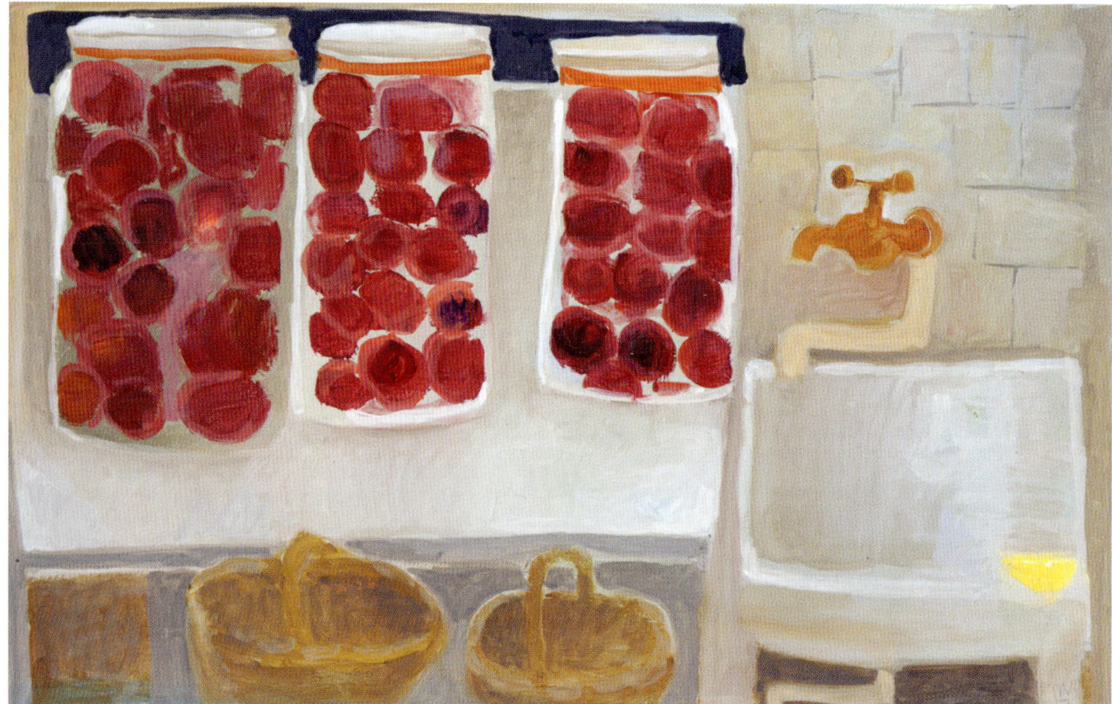

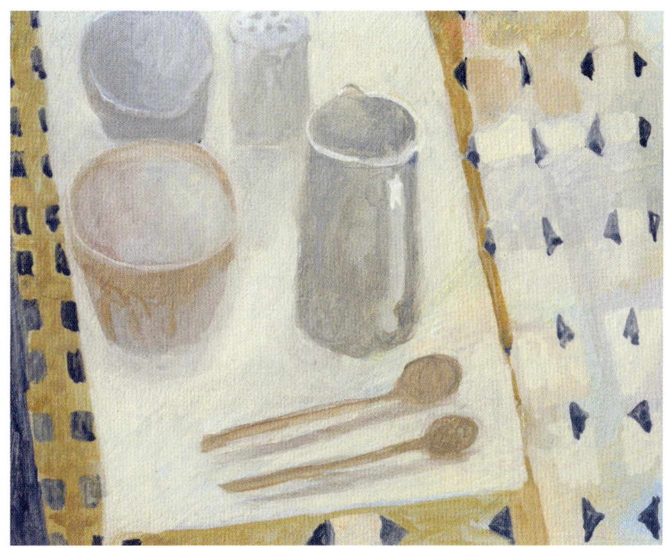

Musée de Camondo (A), 2012
oil on card, 5¾ x 6 ¼ inches

Paris has countless small and bizarre museums... Take the Musée des Cristalleries de Baccarat at number 30 bis rue de Paradis in the tenth arrondissement.... (In the spring this museum should be visited just at closing time when night is beginning to fall and the crystals are glowing dimly in the last shreds of daylight).

(from *The Flâneur: A Stroll through the Paradoxes of Paris* by Edmund White, 2001)

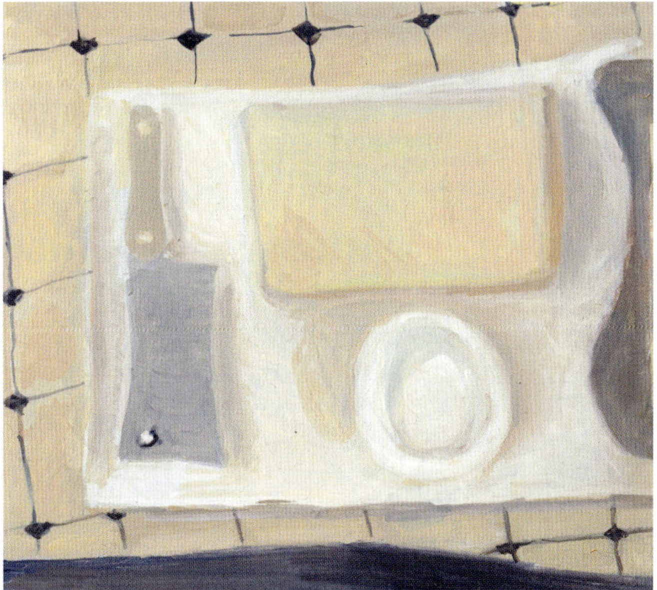

Musée de Camondo (B), 2012
oil on card, 6 x 5¾ inches

Jean Rhys writes of Sasha Jensen, a middle-aged English woman who is staying in a hotel room overlooking rue Lamartine with a little balcony. Emotionally adrift in Paris, she likes it there.

You could stand and lean your arms on the cool iron and look down into the street... The curtains are thin, and when they are drawn the light comes through softly. There are flowers on the window-sill and I can see their shadows on the curtains...

There is a wind, and the flowers on the window-sill, and their shadows on the curtains, are waving. Like swans dipping their beaks in water.
(from Jean Rhys, *Good Morning, Midnight*, 1939)

Shadows of our house played out on the houses across the street. There are our chimney pots. A silver plane crossed the sky. When someone I know is travelling I think they are in the plane I see. My daughter in the sky.

A blind woman is making her way down the street. The shutters opposite are closed.

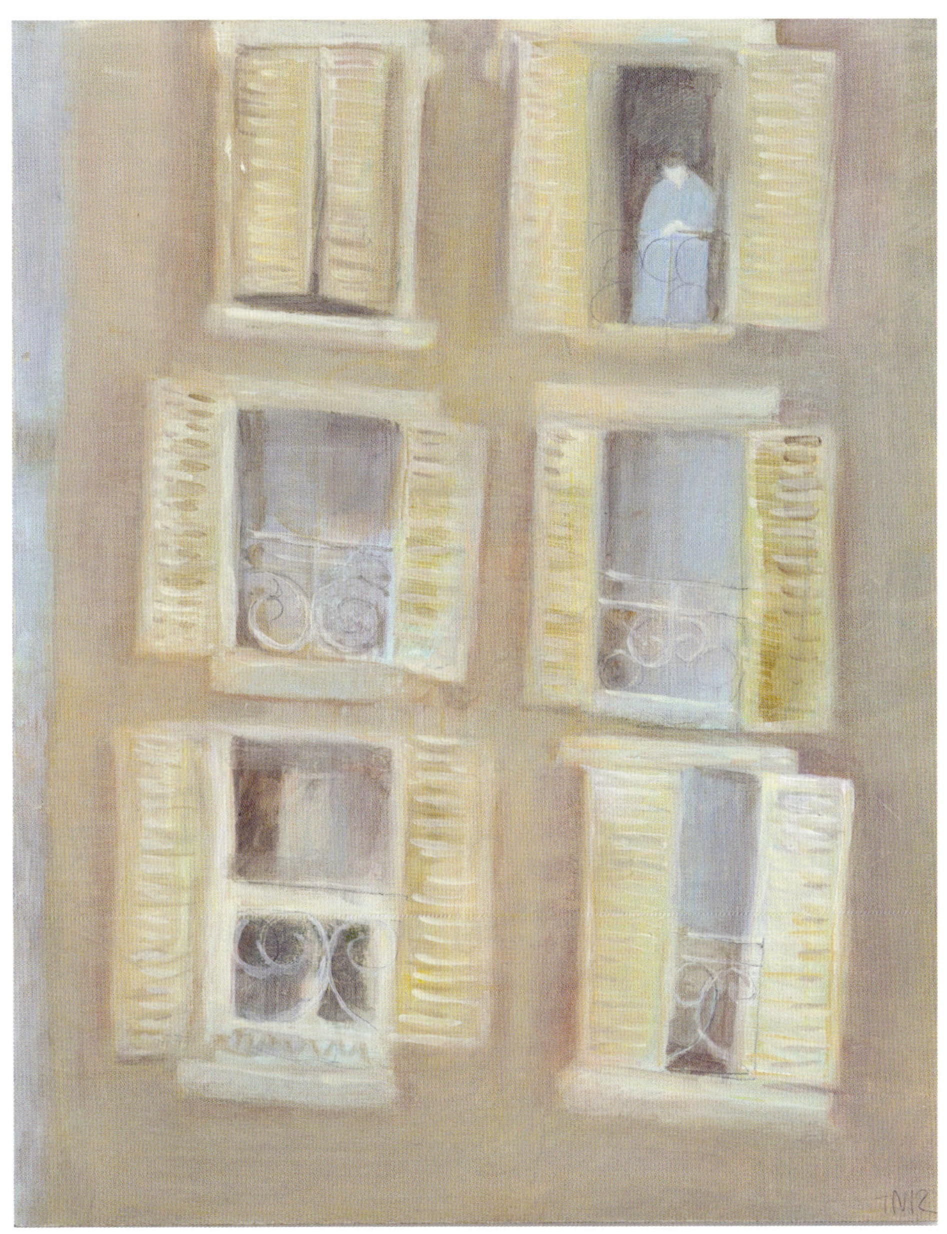

Façade, 2012, oil on board, 11½ x 9 inches

Houses with rows of impassive windows;
They are like blind dogs
The only things that they can see are ghosts.
(from Hope Mirrlees, 'Paris, A Poem', 1919)

Our hotel room

Our hotel is in the north, between stations.
It's very hot. Our window is open. Down in
the street below it's noisy – all night.
The fan turns from side to side. We lie in a
row. Three beds. The *salle de bains* is in a
converted cupboard. It's quite horrid really
but I like being there. In the morning we eat
yoghurt in the courtyard.

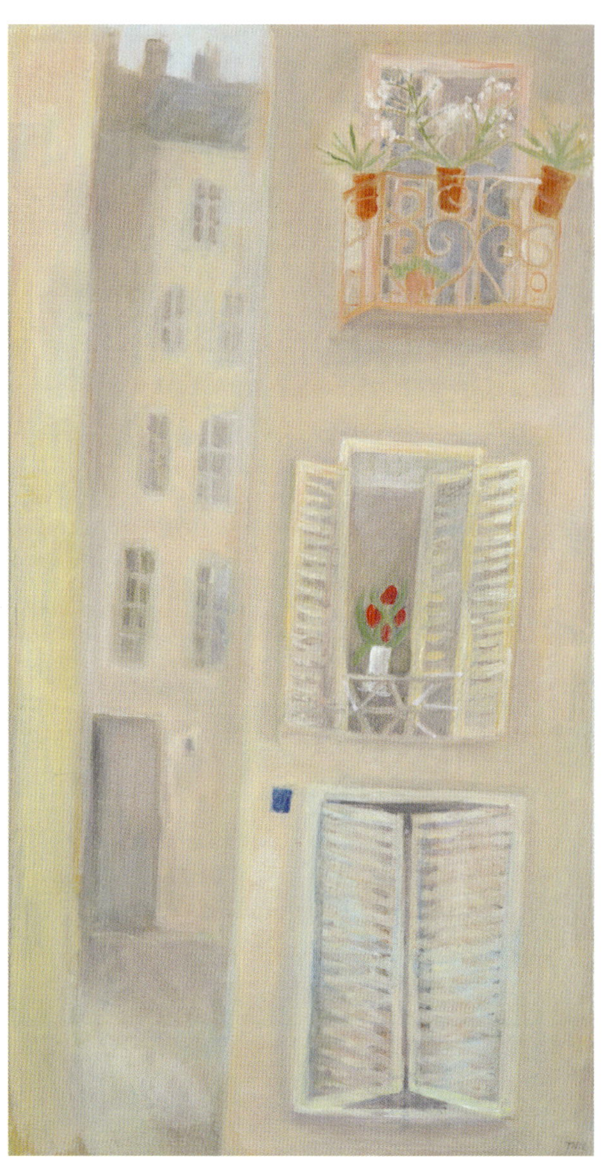

Flowers on Every Stage, 2011, oil on board, 17½ x 8¾ inches

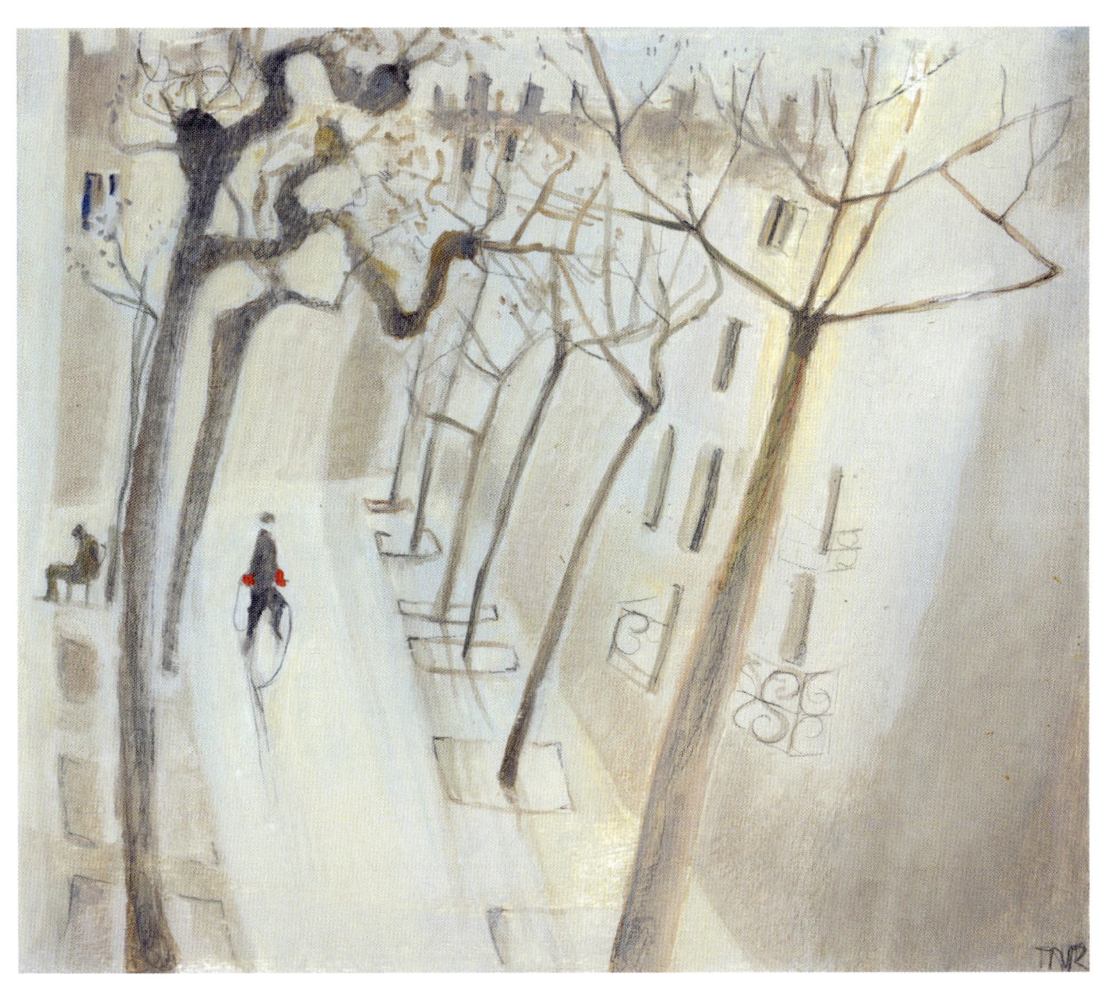

Cycle Lanes, 2012, oil on board, 8 x 8¾ inches

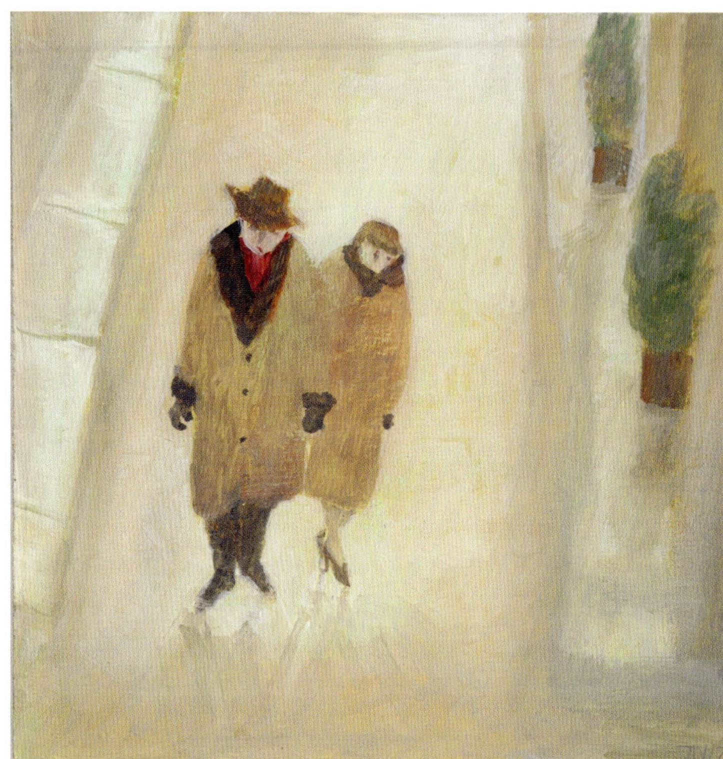

Old, Cold but Still Elegant, 2012
oil on board
7½ x 7 inches

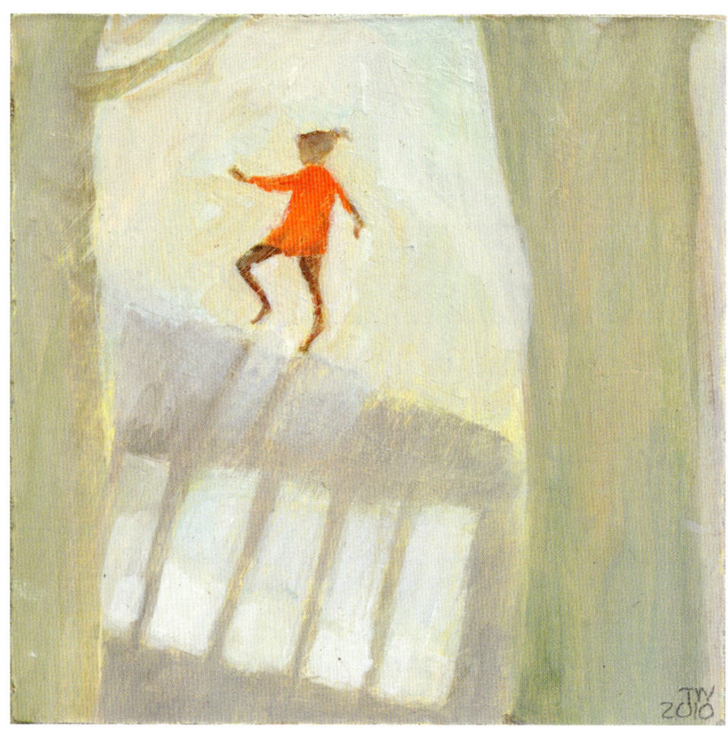

Hopping, 2010
oil on board
4¼ x 4½ inches

CREDITS

The publishers thank the following for granting permission to reproduce copyright material:

Page 18
Parisians: An Adventure History of Paris by Graham Robb, Picador 2010

Pages 34, 41, 45
'Le voyage égoïste' by Colette was published for the first time in 1925
© Librairie Arthème Fayard, 1986

'Journey for Myself', Colette. Translated by David Le Vay. Peter Owen Ltd, London

Pages 42, 43, 53, 64, 66, 69, 91
Hope Mirrlees: Collected Poems, Carcanet Press, 2011

Page 47
Extract from *Le grand Bob* by Georges Simenon reprinted by special permission of Georges Simenon Limited

Page 62
Extract from *Les volets verts* by Georges Simenon reprinted by special permission of Georges Simenon Limited

Page 73
'Jean Cocteau, The Art of Fiction No. 34', interviewed by the author William Fifield in the 'Writers at Work' series, *The Paris Review* (Summer-Fall 1964, No. 32). Reprinted by permission of The William Fifield Collection, Times Two Publishing Company

Pages 81 and 89
The Flâneur: A Stroll through the Paradoxes of Paris © Edmund White 2001. Reproduced by permission of the author c/o Rogers, Coleridge & White Ltd., 20 Powis Mews, London W11 1JN

Page 90
Good Morning, Midnight by Jean Rhys (Penguin Books 1969, reprinted 1975, 1980, 1981, 1984, 1987, reprinted with a new Introduction in Penguin Classics, 2000)
© 1939 by the Estate of Jean Rhys. Introduction © A.L. Kennedy 2000